T0361318

MNEMOSYNE

BIBLIOTHECA CLASSICA BATAVA

COLLEGERUNT

A. D. LEEMAN • H. W. PLEKET • C. J. RUIJGH

BIBLIOTHECAE FASCICULOS EDENDOS CURAVIT

C. J. RUIJGH, KLASSIEK SEMINARIUM, OUDE TURFMARKT 129, AMSTERDAM

SUPPLEMENTUM NONAGESIMUM

J. D. MINYARD

LUCRETIUS
AND
THE LATE REPUBLIC

LUGDUNI BATAVORUM   E. J. BRILL   MCMLXXXV

LUCRETIUS
AND
THE LATE REPUBLIC

LUCRETIUS
AND
THE LATE REPUBLIC

An Essay in Roman Intellectual History

BY

J. D. MINYARD

LEIDEN   E. J. BRILL   1985

ISBN 90 04 07619 0

PRINTED IN THE NETHERLANDS BY E. J. BRILL

CONTENTS

Preface... VII

Lucretius and the Late Republic.. 1

  1. Roman Intellectual History...................................... 1
  2. The *Mos Maiorum* 5
  3. The World and the Late Republic............................... 13
  4. Julius Caesar 15
  5. Catullus 22
  6. Cicero.. 29
  7. Lucretius 33
  8. The Consequences of Crisis.................................... 70

Bibliography.. 80
Index... 84

PREFACE

The genesis of the present study was a paper entitled "Appearances, Reality, and the Formulas of Truth in the Poem of Lucretius," read at the conference on Truth and Reality in Classical Antiquity held at Brown University on 4-6 November 1983. The conference was organized by Professor William F. Wyatt, Jr. of the Brown Classics Department and supported by grants from the National Endowment for the Humanities, the Rhode Island Committee for the Humanities, and the Marshall Woods Lecture Fund of Brown University. Thanks are due to the sponsors, to Professor Wyatt, to Brown University, and to the Brown Department of Classics for the opportunity to present this discussion at an earlier stage of its formulation, the stimulus the conference provided for developing those ideas into a longer treatment, and the kind hospitality afforded me and the other participants, a number of whom made valuable suggestions for improving the argument and exploring its implications. A somewhat different version of the material was then presented on 7 November 1983 as the NEH Faculty Lecture, entitled "The Intellectual Situation of Lucretius," to a seminar consisting of the members of the Department of Classics of Brooklyn College of the City University of New York. Thanks are due to Professor Dee Lesser Clayman, chairman of the department, for her invitation to give the lecture and for the hospitality she and her department provided. Once again, the discussion following the presentation contributed significantly to the improvement of this study.

The present essay is founded in the belief that the true nature of Roman intellectual history has not been fully examined, despite the existence of a number of excellent partial studies and of a wealth of important scholarly treatment of relevant matters from a different point of view (e.g. political or social history). This material can be fruitfully reapplied to the questions of cultural and intellectual history. The essay also rests on the related belief that the study of the actual history of Roman literature and of Lucretius' place in that history is still in its earliest stages, with much fundamental work remaining to be done. The situation is not as bleak as it was even thirty years ago, but the historical treatment of Roman literature as a whole, as opposed to the critical or historical treatment of individual authors, and the notion that Rome had an intellectual life of its own with a history and an impact of its own have yet to have their time of fashion in the history of scholarship. This study is meant to be a step toward relating Lucretius to his specifically Roman cultural context, treating the controversies of the Late Republic as serious intellectual conflicts over the nature, meaning, and direction of Roman society, and constructing a conceptual outline for studying the whole course of Roman intellectual history.

The content of what follows reflects the continuing impact on my outlook of the two earliest sponsors of my Lucretian studies, Michael C. J. Putnam and Phillip H. DeLacy. Many details of the present discussion reflect the benefit I have received from the comments of Professors Giovanni Ferrari, D. J. Furley, Barbara K. Gold, Carl Rubino, Bruce McQueen, Edward Harris, Hardy Hansen, and Howard Wolman, each of whom is owed thanks for several specific improvements.

Greensboro, North Carolina   J. D. M.

LUCRETIUS AND THE LATE REPUBLIC

1. *Roman Intellectual History*

The history of human values is the history of changing notions about truth and reality, however analytically inarticulate those notions may have been. So, the history of values at Rome is a function of the changes in Roman ideas about reality and truth, is, in fact, the core of Roman intellectual history. It is within the framework of this intellectual history, specifically in the context of the struggle over values based upon competing accounts of truth and reality which constitutes the intellectual crisis of the Late Roman Republic, that the *De Rerum Natura* of Lucretius can most powerfully and accurately be understood and, above all, evaluated.

The world in which Lucretius lived, the entire Mediterranean world of the First Century B.C., experienced a crisis as profound as can be imagined absent its elimination. This crisis was general and from it emerged, first, the Augustan arrangement, or *pax*, and, last, the reorientation of life by Christianity. The crisis was, at least, political, military, cultural, and intellectual. It was perhaps also social and economic. At any rate, it had deep consequences for the social and economic organization and content of this world, if it did not alter modes of production and the class framework. It was much more than simply a Roman crisis, but, since, in its last stages before the *pax*, it was a function of the way Rome became the Mediterranean world and the way the Mediterranean world became Rome, in the period of our concern it is distinguishable from the crisis at Rome only conceptually.

This Mediterranean crisis, in its intellectual as well as its other aspects, manifested itself along three fault lines. First was that which ran through the structures of Roman society itself, where movement was produced by the various shocks resulting proximately or ultimately from the process of Roman expansion. Second was one which ran through the societies of the Greek East, movement along which antedated Roman expansion into that area and whose causes can be traced back to the activity of Philip of Macedon and ultimately to internal developments in the old world of the *polis* itself. Movement here was then exacerbated and confirmed by Roman expansion. Third was a line created by the clash between Roman and Hellenistic imperializing cultures, along which occurred the struggle for cultural, intellectual, political, military, and economic dominance, during the last period of Greek influence upon Republican Rome, in the Middle and Late Republics. All three fault lines are evident in the *De Rerum Natura* and can be identified as its historical context, indeed, as its historical causes making this poem a quintessentially Late Republican document, bearing the clear stamp of its cultural environment. It could have come from no other period of Roman history, for Lucretius' poem is the direct product of the genuine crisis of *civitas Romana*.

The world of *civitas*, and with it its account of the way the world works, had been shattered by its own success, and this shattering set its members free to act on their own versions of truth and reality, to find their own sets of values, with the end that, by giving citizens freedom from their citizenship, the crisis cost them the freedom their citizenship had given. *Civitas* had lost its place as the center and source of understanding and purpose, had lost its power to organize life. Only some words and the shells of old habits, which we call the institutions of the Republic and their articulation in law, remained. The old structure of ideas, purposes, and values no longer offered what everyone accepted as the explanation of the nature of things.

Roman imperial expansion, had Hellenic civilization never been, would have produced eventually internal institutional crisis. Because there was such a civilization, because it owned such cultural power, because all Roman history had been characterized by the infusion of Roman life by Hellenic culture, and because Hellenic society had already passed through its own version of this crisis, or was in the last stages of its version, the internal crisis at Rome was worked out ultimately in the forms of Greek experience and became part of the last stage of the general crisis of the Hellenic world. In this sense, the terms in which it was expressed and the basis of the arrangement which contained it, the crisis represented the last step in the Hellenization of Rome.

It is the process of Hellenization, in conjunction with the growth and expansion of Rome, the steps by which Rome was incorporated within the frame of Hellenic culture and the Hellenic and Mediterranean world was reformed by Roman power, that constitutes the framework of Roman intellectual history, just as the model of Hellenic ideas and institutions was the engine of change and the core of its content. It is the perception of this general structure of Roman intellectual history that forms the necessary basis for understanding the structure and tensions of the intellectual life of the Late Republic.

Roman intellectual history up to the end of the Republic divides into five principal stages: (1) the Indo-European heritage of the Italic peoples;

(2) the Italian experience of the Indo-European immigrants (which overlaps all the later stages); (3) the first age of Hellenic influence, during the Regal period, which is closely bound up with Etruscan influence, the two sometimes being the same thing; (4) the second age of Hellenic influence, including the elimination of Etruscan impact, during the Early Republic; (5) the third age of Hellenic influence, resulting from the wide-scale infusion of Roman power into the Greek world and the consequent indiscriminate infusion of Greek culture into Rome, during the Middle and Late Republics. These stages should be as clearly distinguished as evidence and theory allow, and especially should we not speak of Greek influence on Rome as if it were one thing, when the term refers to what were historically three different things, flowing from very different sets of historical circumstances, caused by very different relationships between the two cultures, taking very different forms at each stage, and producing very different results.

There were Greek communities in the Italian peninsula as long as legend and ascertainable fact tell us there was something that could be called a Roman community. The history of Rome as a distinct entity on the banks of the Tiber is coeval with the Greek presence in Italy. Because of its location, and other factors, the Roman community was never isolated from its broader cultural environment. Indeed, the history we can write of its ideas and values is the history of its dealing with external influence. As a result, the separation of the various strands in the structure of Roman ideas and institutions (Indo-European, Italic, Roman, Etruscan, Greek) is extraordinarily difficult. Especially controversial are the separation of Greek elements from Etruscan and the distinction between the direct impact of Greek patterns and that mediated through Etruria. The point important for this study is the antiquity and pervasiveness of the Greek influence. Whatever roles other peoples played in the development of Roman ideas and intellectual life, Greece seems always to have had some impact, and Greek influence was the most various, persistent, profound, and important.

The history of literacy itself at Rome is the history of Greek influence, since the Roman alphabet is the Greek alphabet. In its Etruscan period, if the process had not begun earlier, Rome entered the world of Greek art, architecture, mythology, law, and religion. And it is during the Etruscan era that we can discern clearly the first stages in the Hellenization, i.e. the politicization or civilization, of the City Rome. No important aspect of Roman culture is immune to the imputation of Greek origin or influence, including such features so typically and anciently Roman as the triumph, the Laws of the Twelve Tables, the foundation myths of Romulus and Aeneas, the story (and perhaps the fact) of the expulsion of the "tyrant" Tarquinius Superbus, the inauguration of the institutions of the Republic, and the Saturnian verse. Rome originated on the fringe of Hellenic civilization and was not very old before it was surrounded by the results of the spread of that civilization.[1]

Conclusions important for the consideration of Lucretius flow from these observations. When it is argued that the *De Rerum Natura* represents part of the reaction of its time against the inherited account of the world expressed in the *mos maiorum*, it is not assumed that this tradition of idea and value was itself unaffected by Greek influence or that Greek influence was the new factor causing this reaction. All of Roman history shows the effects of contact with Hellenic culture. What is new in the time of Lucretius, or, actually, in the period of which Lucretius and his con-

---

[1] The study of the early period of the Roman community is notoriously difficult and controversial. Among the most lucid and convenient surveys of the field are A. Momigliano, "An Interim Report on the Origins of Rome", *JRS* 53 (1963) 95-121; the same author's "The Origins of the Roman Republic", Charles S. Singleton (ed.), *Interpretation: Theory and Practice* (Baltimore 1969) 1-34 (particularly 15-18 and 31-32 on Greek influence); and R. M. Ogilvie, *Early Rome and the Etruscans* (Atlantic Highlands, N.J. 1976), including especially the bibliographical essay "Further Reading", 177-184. All the fundamental studies are mentioned by Ogilvie. Particularly relevant to the specific points raised here are: J. Huergon, *The Rise of Rome to 264 B.C.* (London 1973); G. K. Galinsky, *Aeneas, Sicily and Rome* (Princeton 1969); H. Versnel, *Triumphus* (Leiden 1970); and R. Bloch, *The Origins of Rome* (New York 1960), particularly 14, 107-108, 114, 117, 143-148 on Greek influence. In addition to Ogilvie's citations, the following are useful. On the Saturnian verse, see T. Cole, "The Saturnian Verse", *YCS* 21 (1969) 1-73, particularly 46-73, for a survey of the problems of the structure and origin of the meter and of possible influences upon it. On the Roman alphabet, see A. E. Gordon, "On the Origins of the Latin Alphabet: Modern Views", *CSCA* 2 (1969) 157-170, who surveys the scholarship on the question and advocates Etruscan mediation. Whatever the truth, the alphabet is ultimately Greek and an example, direct or indirect, of Greek influence on the world in which Rome lived. Even Gordon admits that how the Romans learned the sound values of certain letters, even if they borrowed the forms from the Etruscans, presents a problem, saying only that they "of course needed them and may somehow have learned their value in Greek" (166). Why not from the Greeks themselves, with whom Romans had early direct contact? There is also a problem associated with the pronunciation of X, the simplest solution of which would appear to be direct encounter with Greeks. Was there no writing on the Greek vases (mostly Attic) imported into Rome all during the Sixth Century B.C. (see Bloch, 89, 92-93, 96, 108)? That hardly seems likely. They will have been important vehicles for direct knowledge of Greek writing. Finally, both Gordon (160) and Ogilvie (49) stress the significance of the Praenestine Fibula as evidence for the proximate Etruscan origin of Roman writing. If, however, Margherita Guarducci's demonstration in *La cosiddetta Fibula Prenestina* (Roma 1980) that the fibula is a Nineteenth Century forgery stands, this document becomes a nullity, and the case for at least partial direct Greek influence is strengthened. Gordon accepts Guarducci in his review of her book, *CJ* 78 (1982) 64-70, with reference to his own article, "The Inscribed Fibula Praenestina, Problems of Authenticity", Univ. Calif. Classic. Studies 16 (1975) 3-24, but no mention of his position in *CSCA*. Since the Romans wrote in the same direction as the Greeks and oppositely from the Etruscans, it might seem likely that the Greeks played a role in teaching the Romans how to write.

temporaries represent the last stage, is the nature, scope, and effect of Greek influence.

The process of which the Rome of the Late Republic was the product and which we usually mean when we speak of the influence of Greece upon Rome, was the third stage of Hellenic influence and was the conversion of Rome into a Hellenistic metropolis, the cosmopolitanization of the *urbs Romana* and ultimately of *civitas Romana*, and has little to do with the fact of Greek influence per se. These are separable features of Roman history. Greek influence, by itself, was independent of Roman expansion. That is, it did not need that expansion to take place. It needed only contact and was, in fact, the product of Greek expansion. This influence was gradual and controllable by the *civitas*. It flowed slowly in channels Rome dug. However Rome might be changed physically and constitutionally, this influence was not overwhelming, in the sense that it threatened the community's basic perceptions and arrangement of itself and its ideas about the nature of reality and hierarchy of values. The third stage of influence required Roman expansion, that is, a fundamental alteration in the objective character of Roman society and the world of which the Romans had experience, such that fundamental alterations in the pattern of Roman life and in Roman ideas became necessary, even inevitable, in order for Rome to manage its objectively different situation. This influence was overwhelming, because the change was so relatively rapid and beyond control, and because the alterations in the Roman world were so both vast and profound. This was the stage of Greek influence that radically threatened the *mos maiorum* and the society it had rationalized and supported.[2]

2. *The Mos Maiorum*

The evolution of the Republic after a century or more of Hellenizing Etruscan rule may be viewed as the second step in the assimilation of Rome to the forms of Hellenic life. In spite of the complexity of the rela-

---

[2] This is the insight offered by Roman historical writers, in their own categories of analysis, when they date the beginning of moral decline at Rome: for example, Livy 39.6.7 on the triumph of Cn. Manlius Vulso (187 B.C.) "de Gallis qui Asiam incolunt" (39.6.3), "Luxuriae enim peregrinae origo ab exercitu Asiatico invecta in urbem est." Also compare 39.6.9: "Vix tamen illa, quae tum conspiciebantur, semina erant futurae luxuriae." Sallust, of course, (*Bellum Catilinae* 11.5) places the beginnings of *luxuria* only in the Asian campaign of Sulla, but in language more suggestive than that of Livy: "Huc accedebat quod L. Sulla exercitum quem in Asia ductaverat, quo sibi fidum faceret, contra morem maiorum luxuriose nimisque liberaliter habuerat." The general decline of the *mos maiorum* Sallust dates from 146 B.C. and the final fall of Carthage (*Bellum Catilinae* 10 and *Bellum Jugurthinum* 41). On this whole topic, see D. C. Earl, *The Political Thought of Sallust* (Cambridge 1961) 41-59.

tion to Hellenism and other outside cultural forces, however, there should be no doubt of the vitality of Rome's tradition and the strength of Roman traditionalism as a value. However various and early the sources of the shape things took eventually, the final structure of institution and idea was distinctively Roman. There was nothing anywhere else in the Mediterranean, after all, exactly like the triumph, the Saturnian verse, the forms of Roman civic practice, or the Roman form of the alphabet.

The commonwealth that emerged from the ruin of royal power was never a static, harmonious community. Its history was often the record of tension, dissension, and sedition.[3] It was, nevertheless, founded on a consistent perception of reality, which was the source of action and its evaluation. This general Roman perception of the nature of the world can be read in the *mos maiorum*, as expressed in the institutions of the Early Republic and their associated vocabulary. This *mos* was the standard to which appeal could be made, the inheritance of custom, procedure, and attitude representing the settled assumptions of shared life, the constitution of the *res publica* which gave form to a *civitas* whose constituted groups might quarrel among themselves, but which formed their judgments on the same account of reality and an agreement about the nature, purposes, and patterns of life. These fundamental perceptions were held in common as the basis of both unity and disunity.

The Classical community, a version of which Rome had become, was both institution and ideal, giving identity, purpose, and value to its members, who, therefore, did not have identity, purpose, or value outside this natural whole of which they were, in their reality, only parts. Education about the world was the observation of how life in the community was led, not schooling in private, secret, speculative analysis. Once a person had learned the forms of community life, had learned what the citizenry considered worthy and unworthy, what was done and what just not done, and what was expected of him according to his rank, age, and sex, he was educated and could become part of the citizenry (*politeia* or *civitas*), a part of the constitution.

In the old-style city, those lines of division characteristic of later society and thought, which reflect, create, and enforce its sense of reality, which are the substance of truth, especially the distinctions between political and religious and military affairs, private and public, individual and society, do not exist. They could not exist. The world of the citizen was not shaped that way. The citizen body was not shaped that way. These

---

[3] The record is set out in P. A. Brunt, *Social Conflicts in the Roman Republic* (New York 1971). See especially Chapter One, "The Background: Roman Expansion and Its Results", for discussion of various aspects of the expansion.

activities and conceptions were not competing centers of value and so were not real entities in the world. Politics, religion, war, person, and family were various and harmonious aspects of the same unitary, undivided reality, different ways and means of achieving the same ends and realizing the same value. Some of these, and related, distinctions did come to exist to a degree in the ancient world, and this development is the large feature of Classical intellectual history, but they are not a part of the analysis of reality embodied in the *mos maiorum*.

The absence in the ancestral commonwealth of distinctions considered fundamental in other forms of thought was both product and cause of the absence of choices assumed to be so natural, real, even inevitable in other ideas of order: choices of career, religion, behavior, dress, language, dwelling, name, association. None of the pressures and none of the openness leading to the individualism so familiar to modern thought were present to any effective degree. Pressures of choice, resulting from openness in the structure of life, produce a sense of self and perception of individuality, indeed, produce the entities "self" and "individual", because there must be some basis on which to choose, some center to which choice is presented and to whose value it can be referred. When that center ceases to be the community, and the agent of choice ceases to be the tradition, then "community" and "tradition" themselves cease to be active categories, however long they may eke out a life as names. The person becomes a separable entity to the extent he becomes the agent of choice and must make his choices on the basis of what he believes he finds inside himself that is different from what he thinks he finds in others. Questions of purpose, value, and identity are no longer purely social and become increasingly personalized. The burden of thinking becomes the identification of the way in which the one is different from the rest. When values are entirely social and external, when the worth of the person, his *dignitas*, is determined by impersonal tradition and is clear to all outside him, because it is not internal and cannot be determined by himself, since he is not a source of value, the burden of thought rests in the assimilation of the one to the many (living, dead, and unborn), or, rather, in the refusal to differentiate person from polity. There are no individuals, only parts of a larger whole. The whole is the unit, the real individual, the true source of thought.

When "individual" and "self" are not centers of value and decision, because they are not categories in the real world, the thought of the person is the thought of the community. The perceptions and mental processes of the part cannot be differentiated from those of the whole. The content of the mind of the citizen is that of the citizenry. Outside citizenry there are no categories of reality or value. The person can have no worth,

no *dignitas*, because worthiness exists as a function of citizenship. There is
no interior life, no world inside, no conception of a separate, personal, internal worth and no way to defend on that basis the citizen against his
citizenship. Thence arises the great dilemma of Achilles in the *Iliad*.
When all value is social and external, the removal of the social, external,
visible signs of value awarded by the community diminishes real value in
the real world, the only value there is, denies the actuality of achievement, and cancels the reason for action and life.

The life that could not be diminished or canceled, the permanent life of
which the activities of persons like Achilles were only a transitory part,
was the life of the community, *ta politika* or *to koinon* for the *polis* and *res
publica* at Rome, where for a sharer in the commonwealth to take a part in
the common life was *versari in re publica*.[4] Community affairs consisted of
all the ways in which the polity dealt with reality and determined the
truth of things. Reality existed in terms of, was assimilated to, the form of
civic life. That is, civic life was considered to be the reflection and
representation of the way of the world. The constitution of the community was a theory of reality and provided both the paradigm of truth and the
method of ascertaining truth. Knowledge of *natura* was gained through
knowledge of the experience of *civitas*, which was distilled in the *mos
maiorum*.

For the Roman community, therefore, the source of knowledge was
the *mos maiorum*, the record of experience in dealing with the world and
the preservation of what had worked and therefore had locked into the
real nature of things. This *mos* was not the *mos senum* or *seniorum*, or
vetustiorum, or *antiquorum*, any one of which it could have been, but
maiorum. The word *maiores* refers to the "ancestors" and to those who are
older than the speaker, but it *means* "those who are greater, who are bigger". This is an embedded evaluation and structuring of experience that
justifies and explains why this *mos* is the true source of knowledge and the
sound test of truth. The expression in Latin is so familiar to us, and this
use of *maiores* in other contexts so common, that we are accustomed to ignore its implication. But it is as profound and pregnant as it is an-
thropologically usual.[5] It structures a relation of present to past, and of

---

[4] See Cicero, *De Re Publica* 1.7 and also the first eight chapters of Book 1 for a wealth of
other idioms for participation in civic life involving *civitas* and *res publica*. Compare *Ad Q.fr.*
3.5.1: "...qui in maximis versatus in re publica rebus essem... ."

[5] See, for example, the suggestive discussion of both *gravitas* and *maiestas* in H. Wagenvoort, *Roman Dynamism* (1947, repr. Westport, Conn. 1976) 104-127. In the present
discussion of words, a sharp distinction is made between "meaning" and "reference" or
"application". The meaning of a word is the principle that links all its references, allows
its various applications, and generates or explains its semantic development. The lexical
method criticized by H. Lloyd-Jones in *The Justice of Zeus* (2nd ed. Berkeley 1983) 2-3,

the future to present and past, that gives a theory of history, social development, and the foundations of ethics, as well as a theory of how knowledge is gained and tested. It stems from the notion that knowledge is social in acquisition and form, not the product of private, internal, historically and politically unrooted contemplation and speculation. Unless we measure the force of this assumption in its impact on thought and perception of value, we shall not be able to account fully for its power as a positive impulse to action, a terrific barrier to innovation, and a feature defining the struggle to respond and the terms of the response of Roman intellectuals as the Roman experience of the world changed so radically in the period of expansion beyond Italic lands. The heritage of belief was that the *maiores* had locked into reality by discovering the proper formula, the binding spell, the *ius* of things and the modes of action the *ius* entails. By finding the right chant, incantation, spell, or bond of ritual that gives access to the way of the world, they had found the principal or structure of the world and so gained some control over it.[6] Thus attuning themselves to that aspect of reality more powerful than they, they secured the well-being (*salus*) of the *civitas* and fashioned that *pax deorum* which is the proper alignment between the human and divine elements of the community. *Ius* is the key to reality and leads to the notions expressed in *iustus*, *iustitia*, *iniuria*, *coniuratio*, *iudex*, *ius naturale*, and *bellum iustum* (ritual or formulaic war). Knowledge of the *ius* will allow the prescription and proscription (*lex*) of forms of action, the picking out of what is to be done and not done in our relation with other human beings. In our dealing with divinity, it will enable us to see what is *fas* and *nefas*, a fundamental bifurcation in the real world, just as our categories of "blessed" and "damned" represent a dichotomy explicitly denied by the theory of the *mos*, as expressed in its adjective *sacer*.

In addition to *res publica*, *civitas*, *dignitas*, *deus*, *ius*, *lex*, *salus*, *sacer*, *fas*, and *nefas*, the other principal categories of the *mos maiorum* are familiar: *virtus*, *pietas*, *religio*, *fides*, *gloria*, *laus*, *honor*, *auctoritas*, *gravitas*, *severitas*, *nobilitas*, *pater/patronus/patria*, *senatus*, *populus*, *cliens*, *plebs*, *pax*, *foedus*, *bellum*, *gens*, *familia*, *beneficium*, *officium*, *imperium*. These terms are social and refer to external, observable conduct and position. They are not abstract (even when personified, which is not the same as abstraction)

157-158, and 165-167, is deficient not only in its limitation to the study of vocabulary, if that is a deficiency in the study of the way in which a people analyzes and understands its experience, but more seriously in its equation of use and meaning, such that meaning becomes a function of use rather than its explanation. Use flows from meaning, not meaning from use.

[6] On the religious background of *ius*, see, e.g., L. R. Palmer, *The Latin Language* (London 1951) 25-26 (also on *lex*) and A. Ernout-A. Meillet, *Dictionnaire Étymologique de La Langue Latine* (4th ed. Paris 1959), *s.v.*

and do not designate internal qualities or states of being. While most of
the foregoing words became abstracted in later Latin and in the later
history of civilization, in the early period they were not terms of the in-
tellectualization of experience, abstract conclusions drawn away from the
tangible and perceived world, but the visible things of the available
world. They were not rationalizations of the world but terms of the first
order, true names and true things. And they were not only names for the
behavior of men and the working of the world that it was possible to see
and which had been seen, they were also parts of a coherent system for
understanding the whole of the world and cannot be understood as terms
in isolation from one another. They are interdependent, each drawing
from the others its referential power, its moral significance, and its
analytic vitality. *Pietas* and *religio* validate each other, as do *honor*, *gravitas*,
severitas, *gloria*, *virtus*, and *nobilitas*. *Senatus*, *populus*, *cliens*, *patronus*, *patres*,
gens, and *familia* also coexist in a firm and closed structure, each gaining
its meaning and function from the other aspects of that structure. They
have ńo independent roles. All the terms of the *mos* together create a
whole consistently and clearly articulated world. Bringing together
knowledge, society, and nature, they are public, traditional, communal,
and independent of personal perception or individual judgment.

In such an intellectual setting, highest value was placed on the whole
community itself, therefore, upon the loyalty, the being true, the *pietas*, of
the parts to the whole on which they depended for their reality: to family,
to communal city, to divinity which governed the whole. *Pietas* was the
active and positive side of negative *religio*. Each was the injunction of
divinity regarding those forms of life it sanctioned. Excellence in *pietas*,
based on observance of *religio* and a consciousness of *ius* as exposed in the
mos maiorum, was *virtus*, manliness or the forms of manhood. *Virtus* was,
like the other terms, a pattern of performance, not an inner quality, ex-
isting only in noticeable achievement—noticeable, hence noble or *nobilis*.
This was what made a man known, known in the right way, and becoming known so was the great goal, the attainment of *nobilitas*, upon which
eventually membership in the group of power was founded, the group of
the *nobiles*, the famous section of the citizenry. The worth these people
were judged to have, the worth they showed and which made them
known, was measured by the distinctions they had deserved and been
awarded by the community, their *honores*. These *honores* were the elements
of their *dignitas*, their real worth in the civic world, their standing among
their fellow citizens, their rank in the *civitas*. These *honores* and this *dignitas*
proceeded from and produced their *auctoritas*, their ability to increase
their patrimony. *Auctoritas* is also social and refers to accomplishment,
which can be seen and the results of which can be seen. The people who

were the sort most seriously to be engaged in such service of augmenta-
tion, to desire this achievement and be fashioned by it, were those who
revealed and developed seriousness itself, weightiness, *gravitas*. *Gravitas*
was both precondition and product of merit, i.e. service to family, polity,
and divinity. By such performance and sanctification, a man became
after his death one of the bigger ones, one of the *maiores*.

The entire world of the citizen was thus represented in the constitution
(*mos maiorum*) of the community (*res publica*). Truthfulness (*pietas*) to the
fellowship of the citizens (*civitas*) brought *gloria* in the *laudes* of their fellows
to those who showed they were men (*virtus*). The cohesion of this hierar-
chical fellowship was secured by the performance of *beneficia* and *officia*.
This was the original familial nexus of *patronus* and *cliens* from which civil
society grew, itself flowing from the model of *pater* and *familia*, and which
formed the original *populus*, the *classis* to which accessory elements in the
city (*plebs*) later clamored for admittance, and which they were in the end
allowed to fill out. Various stages of civil tension and disaster brought the
incorporation by steps of the *plebs*, who then became part of and could
fight in defense and extension of *imperium*. The values inherent in the notion of *maiores* had made the *senes* preeminent, perhaps in the very earliest
stages of the regal form of the society, and so counsel was at some point
located in a *senatus*, chosen from those who could be called *patres*, the
nucleus or origin of that rank called *patricius*. The warrant that
demonstrated the truthfulness of a relationship or word was in action, the
link between words and things, that credit or guarantee, was *fides*,
something public, testable, social, and observable because it took its life
in deeds and events and referred to that active, visible bond in the working of the world expressed in the forms of polity.

What individualism there was in the world of the *mos maiorum*, i.e. the
kind of thing which, according to the categories of the modern analysis of
reality, we call individualism, assimilating and warping the Roman
perception to fit our own, lay in the degree of excellence of service to the
community among the *nobiles*, the degree of assimilation to and ex-
emplification of inherited patterns that led to *nobilitas*. The system of
social value, like the social system it reflected and justified, was oligarchic. Each rank had obligation and value, but the rank of great value,
whose members were not personally obscure, was that which had the
nobilitas. All ranks recognized this hierarchy as the natural order of
things. The more a person stood out from the members of his class in the
virtue of his merits, i.e. the more he might seem an individual in the
categorizations of our language, the less he stood forth from his class, the
more he expressed its standards, the more a part of the group he became.
The more individually excellent he might seem to us, the less an in-

dividual he was to his classmates. The paradox exists only in terms of our words and the analysis they reflect, not in terms of the organization of reality found in the Classical community. It is a point worth noting because of what was to happen to the cohesion within and between the classes by the Late Republic, particularly the fissures in the oligarchic order. These fissures and their results in the life of the words of the *mos maiorum* (e.g. *virtus, pietas, nobilitas, dignitas, auctoritas, religio, iustus*) comprise the substance of Roman intellectual history and provide the necessary foundation for understanding the dimensions and meaning of what happened.[7]

---

[7] This extremely abbreviated outline of the *mos maiorum*, its social origin and reference, its implications, and its effects in the world of action can be fleshed out, with appropriate modification and documentation, in a number of important works whose aim is primarily political history but which lay the foundation of the study of Roman intellectual culture. First may be noted the classic account of Fustel de Coulanges, *La Cité Antique*, which, in spite of the subversion of its history by later scholarship, gives a vivid and accurate picture of the total interfusion of religion, family, and social form in the Classical community and that coherent civic intellectual framework which was its cause and product. The opening sentence of Fustel's first chapter establishes the point of view underlying the present discussion: "Jusqu'aux derniers temps de l'histoire de la Grèce et de Rome, on voit persister chez le vulgaire un ensemble de pensées et d'usages qui dataient assurément d'une époque très-éloignée et par lesquels nous pouvons apprendre quelles opinions l'homme se fit d'abord sur sa propre nature, sur son âme, sur le mystère de la mort." (*La Cité Antique* [Paris 1927] 7.) Foremost among more recent works are: W. V. Harris, *War and Imperialism in Republican Rome: 327-70 B.C.* (Oxford 1979), especially 10-41; R. E. A. Palmer, *The Archaic Community of the Romans* (Cambridge 1970), especially 41-44, 157-160, 197-202, 230-232, and elsewhere for suggestive discussion of Roman categories of analysis and the social form of Roman thought; E. Badian, *Foreign Clientelae (264-70 B.C.)* (Oxford 1958), particularly for the discussion of *beneficium/officium*, 154-167, and in general for the embodiment of political thought in institution and action; the same author's *Roman Imperialism in the Late Republic* (2nd ed.; repr. Ithaca 1971), especially Chapter 1, "*Virtus* and *Imperium*", 1-15, for an analysis of basic categories and such observations as, "... in Rome, when an unusual situation arose, it was natural to consult *mos maiorum*..." (22); M. Gelzer, *The Roman Nobility*, trans. R. Seagar (Oxford 1969), especially 65-69 (on *fides* and related terms) and 27-40 on "nobility"; L. R. Taylor, *Party Politics in the Age of Caesar* (Berkely 1949), especially 1-24, 41-42, 76-97, 162-182; R. Syme, *The Roman Revolution* (Oxford 1939), especially 10-27 and 149-161; D. C. Earl, *The Political Thought of Sallust* (Cambridge 1961), especially the two chapters on *virtus*, 18-40, and R. Syme, *Sallust* (Berkeley 1964), for discussion of the traditional categories in the Late Republic; also, S. Weinstock, *Divus Julius* (Oxford 1971), especially 133-135, 167-169, 230-259, 267-269. Literary analyses pertinent to this history of the *mos maiorum* are, e.g., E. Segal, *Roman Laughter: The Comedy of Plautus* (Cambridge, Mass. 1968), especially 15-41, and D. Konstan, *Roman Comedy* (Ithaca 1983), especially 33-46, 57-72, and 73-95. There are, of course, some works devoted specificially to the history of ideas at Rome, including: F. E. Adcock, *Roman Political Ideas and Practice* (Ann Arbor 1964), especially 3-35, and Adcock cites the fundamental studies of the key terms of the *mos maiorum*, distilling the scholarship on these points up to the date of publication, but those studies, as indicated in Note 5 above, proceed from a different conception of the meaning of a word from that offered here; M. L. Clarke, *The Roman Mind* (New York 1968), especially 8-31 and 42-53; and D. Earl, *The Moral and Political Tradition of Rome* (Ithaca 1967), especially 11-43. An important discussion of a major portion of the history of Roman thought and its relationship to

3. The World and the Late Republic

The structure of idea and value embodied in the Classical Roman *civitas* had been under pressure for some considerable time by the 50's B.C. Imperial expansion into the Mediterranean world, the influx of wealth, importation of slaves in large numbers, the growth of foreign populations at Rome, the fighting of large-scale and prolonged wars outside Italy, expanded opportunity for personal aristocratic adventure and enrichment, the vast increase in personal power through what had started out to be community service, the consequent changing bases of power, the treatment accorded conquering generals in the kingdoms of the East, increasing acquaintance with alien philosophies and religions, the Hellenization (the institutionalization) of education—all this, and more, exacerbated divisions within and between classes, offered alternatives of value, opportunity, and idea to the inherited community service, loosened the bond of community by creating a world unable to be comprehended by the civic rationale, caused many of the old assumptions about reality to seem naive and inadequate, and through these and related processes fashioned positive and negative stimuli which combined

---

political and social history is Ch. Wirszubski, *Libertas as a Political Idea at Rome During the Late Republic and Early Principate* (Cambridge 1950), particularly Chapter 3: "The Decline of the Traditional Form of Government." Most instructive for the assumptions and thrust of this essay, however, are two books which are real treatises on intellectual history, even though they are concerned with Roman history subsequent to the Late Republic (but also, and this helps to make them so instructive, as consequent upon the crisis of the Late Republic): C. G. Starr, *Civilization and the Caesars* (1954; repr. New York 1965), especially 3-30, and C. N. Cochrane, *Christianity and Classical Culture* (rev. ed. 1944; repr. Oxford 1968), especially 27-61. There are, of course, many other studies devoted to the background material of this essay, some of which will be noted later in particular contexts, but those cited indicate where information lies, and what its significance is. It is, however, useful to mention here A. Thornton, *The Living Universe: Gods and Men in Virgil's Aeneid* (Leiden 1976) 1-34, for a description of the picture of the universe of the First Century B.C. particularly relevant to Lucretius as an account of the world view among the educated which provides the *De Rerum Natura* with a direction and relevance generally neglected in treatments of *religio* and related themes in Lucretius' poem. It may be also noted that a good ancient account of the world out of which the *res publica Romana* emerged and which was expressed in the *mos maiorum*, the power of its key words and the lack of that structure of distinctions with which we are familiar, is contained in the *Germania* of Tacitus. This monograph shows the utility of the traditional terms as categories of analysis, how they shape his perception of the Germanic experience and conform it to the world of Latin. While his subject is the Germans, his descriptions apply equally, if not sometimes better, to the attitudes and values of early Rome, e.g.: "Nihil autem neque publicae neque privatae rei nisi armati agunt. sed arma sumere non ante cuiquam moris quam civitas suffecturum probaverit. tum in ipso concilio vel principum aliquis vel pater vel propinqui scuto frameaque iuvenem ornant: haec apud illos toga, his primus iuventae honos; *ante hoc domus pars videntur, mox rei publicae.* insignis nobilitas aut magna patrum merita principis dignationem etiam adulescentulis adsignant" (13.1-2). *Mutatis mutandis,* this is Rome and the ancient *mos.*

to separate person from polity and replicate in a Roman context the disintegrative and deracinatory experience of the old Hellenic polities.[8] This time, however, because of the nature of the relationship between Greece and Rome, as well as the reformation of the Mediterranean world by Roman power and the enrichment of Roman power by Mediterranean exigency and example, the crisis reached into every corner of the Classical world.

The enrichment of Roman civic life, economically and culturally, shredded the fabric of civic reality and caused the rise of a non-civic individualism. Because the old form of knowledge was rooted in social categories and values, anything that happened to the form of society was necessarily intellectual in consequence. Intellectual crisis flowed then from the collapse of the categories of the polity and the conflicting attempts of force and thought to reshape the account of reality and value according to new experience. By the 50's B.C., therefore, it was necessary even for the Old Believers to defend the inherited account of reality and value, because nothing could be taken for granted. The *mos maiorum* has become, by virtue of circumstances, paradoxically as personal as its rivals, for the choice to uphold it rested now upon individual decision and reflected an individual hierarchy of goals and values. The very defense of the civic system entailed confession of its demise in the old form.

This change in the nature of the objective experience of the citizen and his knowledge of the world put an especial strain on the old ideas, because the new activity and the new world were dressed in the old language. The old words for purpose and value remained, when purposes and values had changed, and new categories were given the old names. Since the old words no longer always designated the same realities they had in days gone by, the separation between words and things widened, and the question of truth, of *fides*, became of paramount importance. Words were released from their anchor in an agreement about reality, names from the sets they named, when the sets were fundamentally altered or had perhaps ceased to exist, and it became nearly impossible to tell whether a term was being used to name the things it had

---

[8] The intellectual significance of the demise of the autonomous *polis* and the Hellenistic period of Greek history in the view of this essay is shown, e.g., by G. Murray, *Five Stages of Greek Religion* (3rd ed. 1951; repr. New York N.D.) 119-165; J. B. Bury, "The Hellenistic Age and the History of Civilization", 1-30, and E. Bevan, "Hellenistic Popular Philosophy", 79-107, in *The Hellenistic Age* (Cambridge 1923); F. W. Walbank, *The Helllenistic World* (Cambridge 1982), especially 86 and 141-158 on the new-style cities and 176-197 on developments in philosophy and science. Particularly germane to the present subject are B. Farrington, *Science and Politics in the Ancient World* (New York 1940) 87-129 and *The Faith of Epicurus* (New York 1967) 63-92.

originally named, was being expanded legitimately to take account of new perceptions of reality, or was simply being used as an empty slogan to disguise reality by lying about new things with old words. The form in which the crisis worked itself out can be represented by many examples, but the most significant and typical, for this age and for their consequences in later generations, were the career, ideas, and ambitions of Julius Caesar, the career, writings, and intellectual accomplishment of Cicero, the poems and the ethic of Catullus, and the poem and the challenge of Lucretius.

4. *Julius Caesar*

Whatever Caesar's specific aims at the various points of his career, the concern of the present discussion is with the fact that his career took its strength and shape from the divorce of perceptions of reality from the terms available in the inherited discourse for those perceptions. These terms had come by and during the lifetime of Caesar to be used as tools for manipulating the reactions of others as much as for the expression of knowledge. They became the instruments of "politics" in our sense of the word, a category which had now come to exist in a form at Rome but which had little to do with the ancestral conception of *versari in re publica*. Caesar's cavalier treatment of his colleague Bibulus, his contempt for the forms of religious belief and the expression of religious power, his Hellenizing reforms and categories of expression, his arrangements with Pompey and Crassus, his treatment of the expansion of citizenship and the Senate, and even his reform of the calendar not only flow from a cosmopolitan rationalizing cynicism but are among the most obvious examples of the link between idea, action, and social form at Rome.

Caesar's cosmopolitanism, rationalism, and cynicism, and their necessary consequence in his political practice, is striking evidence of the degree to which the world of ideas at Rome and the possiblities for action had changed, even from the state of affairs in the age of Marius. His disdain for the restraints of polity was far more suggestive and much more far-reaching than that of the brute self-seeking of so many of his fellows because it was much more intellectualized, much more the product of analysis and theory, as well as of the greater variety of low opportunity. He was intellectually much the superior of most of his contemporaries and predecessors in the search for power, deeply trained in the ways of Hellenistic thought, and gifted with more historical insight than he was perhaps ultimately able to handle. His actions reveal a calculating, Hellenizing mind that has made its decision about the account of the world supplied by the *mos maiorum* and knows the alternative sources of action supplied both by the forms of Eastern power and competing systems of analysis.

The most obvious example of Caesar's true attitude is his fantastic assertion of his *dignitas* on crossing the Rubicon.[9] *Dignitas* as a category of reality had emerged from the communal world of the *civitas*, as the foundation of oligarchy and oligarchic rule. It is worth assigned by citizenry on the basis of service to citizenship. It is ancestral, social, and oligarchic in form and content, not individual and private. It is a function of participation in community and cannot be cited as the cause for war on the community, since destruction of the social framework abolishes the social value. It cannot be claimed as motivation for defiance of community and contempt of its edict, if the person using it still believes in the account of reality on which it is predicated. As part of the structure of social knowledge, it exists only insofar as the mind of a person, the content and processes of his thought, is not distinguished or distinguishable from the processes and content of the thought of the community. It cannot be the instrument of personal thought, because it is the evaluation of person by community and has reality only as an instrument of collective thought, of the denial of individual reality and the reality of the individual.

If Caesar had really believed in the traditional content of the term, if he had been a Republican oligarch in fact as in name, he could have used the argument from *dignitas*, as Achilles asserted the heroic equivalent, by withdrawal from a group that denied his observed and observable worth by retracting what it had previously granted, thus denying its own standards and process. The careers of Scipio Major and Lucullus were models of this. Whatever complicating factors were present in these and similar instances, the infringement of a *dignitas* still believed in as a social value was certainly an intelligible and authentic motivation for withdrawal. Or, Caesar could simply have submitted to the social edict, fighting the

---

[9] Suetonius, *Julius* 33; Caesar, *Bellum Civile* 1.7.5 (and all of 1.7). M. Gelzer, *Caesar: Politician and Statesman*, 6th ed. trans. P. Needham (Oxford 1968), points out (50) that Caesar did not "attack as unconstitutional the decree that was directed against himself in 49." On 189, Gelzer comments that Caesar wanted the support of the Senate and "wished to avoid war if only he could maintain his *dignitas*." But *dignitas*, when it was a reality, was a social form, the product of social order, and could therefore neither be self-asserted nor defended *against* social order. Another discussion of Caesar's career and the categories of the *mos maiorum* is E. Wistrand, *Caesar and Contemporary Society* (Göteborg 1978). See especially 28-32 on Caesar's allegation of *dignitas*. The replies of Pompey and Cicero quoted by Wistrand on 30-31 are, however self-serving, the genuine rebuke to Caesar of the Old Believers, for whom *dignitas* is still a thing and not a name alone, and Wistrand (31-32) aptly cites Sallust's account of Catiline's assertion of his *dignitas* as a cause for his rebellion. The Catilinarian claim was simply phony and is the adequate sign of the worth of Caesar's assertion, from the point of view of the *mos maiorum*. See also Wirszubski (above, note 7) 74-79.

matter out in the oligarchic pattern. What he could not do was assert his *dignitas* as a reason for opposing constitutional behavior, unless he had already determined that there was no such thing as constitutional behavior and that all allegations of it were pretexts as empty as his own. Employment of a term as a propagandistic pretext for defying what one has already decided is a false category can only be intended to fool the thoughtless, confuse issues, and disguise real motivation. Clearly Caesar no longer lived in the world of civic reality, the world as defined by *civitas*, as perhaps no one else in his time did either.

In what world, then, had Caesar come to live? The question brings us to the point of his association with Epicureanism.[10] Caesar was not a philosopher. He was not a professional speculative thinker. He was a man of action in a world of imperial ambition, known for his coolness, cynicism, and easy ruthlessness. But he was intellectual, well-educated, one of the finest of the Republican prose stylists, a distinguished orator in a world where rhetoric was an authentic and respected mode of thought, the composer of historically valuable and astute memoirs, the author of a treatise on grammatical theory, and the composer of a rebuke of Cato's memory that showed understanding of the power of ideas and the importance of intellectual symbolism. A masterful manipulator of language, he was at his ease with the intellectual fashions of the salons of the high life of Roman culture and recognized their utility as the framework and potential servants of his ambition.

No one makes decisions except on the basis of assumptions about the nature of reality and value, however inarticulate and crude his analysis may be. This is true of a Hitler, a Mussolini, a Stalin. However ruthless and cynical we may argue a man with tastes so intellectual as Caesar's to

---

[10] On the connection of Caesar with Epicureans, see N. W. DeWitt, *Epicurus and His Philosophy* (Minneapolis 1954) 343; A. D. Winspear, *Lucretius and Scientific Thought* (Montreal 1963) 20, 40, 71-73; A. Momigliano, review of Farrington's *Science and Politics in the Ancient World, JRS* 31 (1941) 149-157; Sallust, *Bellum Catilinae* 51.19-21, discussed below; Cicero, *Ad Fam.* 15.19.3 (on Pansa), 7.12 (on the conversion of Trebatius), and 11.28 (from Matius on the assassination of Caesar). Farrington, *Science and Politics*, 183-185, misses the point of Caesar's Epicurean argument in Sallust, where Caesar's statement does not need to be explained away as evidence against the power of *religio Romana* but to be appreciated as an extraordinary confession of an unusual point of view. On Caesar's religious reforms, see of course S. Weinstock, *Divus Julius* (above, note 7), but also the review of R. E. A. Palmer, *Athenaeum* 51 (1973) 201-213, who seems to me to take a much sounder view of the matter. Weinstock gives much valuable information on Roman traditions and ideas and the world which Caesar was manipulating. What he demonstrates is not Caesar's sincerity but the world of ideas Caesar was consciously using for his own purposes (how he could get away with so much): the degree to which Rome was becoming a new-style city and Caesar's awareness of his goals. As Palmer comments (203): "the absence of much religiosity from Caesar's writings may tell us something about his sincerity."

be, with a manner so refined and celebrated for its finesse, we argue that he was able to be so cynical and ruthless because this was what his world of ideas allowed. He could not have acted as he did, had he taken the inherited account of the world seriously, had he not thought very differently of what there was for him to fear and what he could laugh at without a care for consequences. Had he placed much credence in Stoicism, or in Platonic or Aristotelian versions of reality, value, reward, punishment, and the aim of life, his conduct would have been different. Indeed, if we were to speculate on the intellectual sources of Caesar's life, without any other information about his age or about his associations and beliefs, we could easily say that he exhibited in action the tenets of an Epicurean physics uprooted from Epicurean ethics. Acceptance of Epicurean mechanical materialism and disregard of Epicurean moral conclusions would give someone a great field for action in the world, freeing him from fear and laying on him no obligations except to his own rationalizing sophistication.

A good deal about the intellectual climate of the Late Republic and Caesar's associations allow the case to be defined more closely. This was the one period in Roman history when Epicureanism, a system so uncongenial to Roman institutions and unsuited to the fundamental motivations of that society, gained anything like respectability and popularity.[11] That it was a prominent and significant feature of Late Republican intellectual life the writings of Lucretius and Cicero, the mention of so many lost Epicurean treatises, the career of Philodemus, the school at Naples, and the association of so many names with its ideals show. The existence of so may "parlor Epicureans", attracted to the Garden, but scarcely schoolmen, let alone true practitioners outside the rhetoric of their own salons, is a good indication of the degree to which the doctrine had penetrated the contemporary Roman world of ideas as both fashion and challenge. There was interest in the system among Caesar's lieutenants in Gaul, where Pansa was a devotee, Trebatius was converted, and Q. Cicero read and corresponded with his brother about Lucretius. Piso, Epicurean and patron of Philodemus, was Caesar's father-in-law.

---

[11] On the history of Epicureanism at Rome, see in particular: N. W. De Witt, *Epicurus and His Philosophy* (above, note 10) 340-358; B. Farrington, *Science and Politics* (above, note 8) 160-216 and *The Faith of Epicurus* (above, note 8) 136-143; M. L. Clarke, *The Roman Mind* (above, note 7) 19-31; H. M. Howe, "Amafinius, Lucretius, and Cicero", *AJP* 72 (1951) 57-62, and "Three Groups of Roman Epicureans", *TAPA* 79 (1948) 341-342; W. Allen, Jr. and P. H. DeLacy, "The Patrons of Philodemus", *CP* 34 (1939) 59-65; P. H. DeLacy, "Cicero's Invective Against Piso", *TAPA* 72 (1941) 49-58; and most especially A. Momigliano's review of Farrington (above, note 10).

It is easy to understand the prominence of Epicureanism in this age. The founder and his followers had seen their Greek cities go through political and intellectual changes comparable to those taking place at Rome. The system was a coherent and detailed response to the events and developments which had undermined the world of the *polis*. The flaws exposed in the political inheritance had led Epicurus to reject the life of the *polis* as the framework for human thought in the belief that that life had been shown to be corrupt by its nature, because it was founded on an erroneous conception of the world and man's place in it. It was natural that when Rome passed through similar trials, the Epicurean answer should find its audience, particularly when the dangers and frustrations of active participation in civic life increased so strikingly.

The scientific sophistication of Epicureanism, its cool disdain for excessive emotionalism, its contempt for superstition and mere traditionalism, its dismissal of the crudities of ancient religion, its comfortable cosmopolitanism, and its clear-headed perception of the follies of life and politics would have had strong appeal to someone of Caesar's temperament and cast of mind. Even if he could not take seriously its call to the obscure life and a contented passivity, its dismissal of the forms and values of the *polis* would have accorded with his own evident perception of the trends of history, as his political, military, and religious policies show, and its physical and epistemological hypotheses would have supported well the style and aim of his reform, even if it could not have brooked his manipulation of popular religious ideas.

Whatever the details of Caesar's thought, the picture Sallust gives of his framework of ideas in the narration of his debate with Cato the Younger in the *Bellum Catilinae* conforms to the description offered here and thus, at least, to the public perception of the man and his values. This is, indeed, Sallust's great value for our purpose. We need not accept the accuracy of his account of the discussion of the punishment of the Catilinarian conspirators in detail in order to appreciate the accuracy of the portrait he draws of the climate of ideas in the Late Republic. The debate between Cato and Caesar presents a paradigm of Late Republican intellectual and political conflict. The use of inherited terms of analysis, the argument over notions of truth and falsity, the relation between words and things, and the impact of Hellenistic philosophizing at a time of intense civil crisis lie at the bottom of both speeches.

Caesar's argument is a smooth rationale for declining to execute the conspirators, employing the standard appeals to historical precedent and the good of the commonwealth. Significant is the beginning, in which he argues against indulgence of the passions, particularly *ira* and *odium*, whose centrality to his point he attempts to veil by citing *amicitia* and *misericordia* as well, because they get in the way of the perception of truth and the service of utility: "haud facile animus verum providet, ubi illa officiunt, neque quisquam omnium lubidini simul et usui paruit." (*BC* 51.2.) This is an argument consonant with the commonplaces of Hellenistic philosophy, including Epicureanism. It does not express the point of view either of Cato's speech, yet to come, or the four speeches of Cicero against the conspirators, in both of which the appeal to patriotic emotion, fear, and devotion to inherited values is central. Caesar goes on to belittle, in effect, the appeals to emotion made by other speakers as irrelevant to decision and then makes a remarkable argument about the irrelevance of execution as punishment: "De poena possum equidem dicere, id quod res habet, in luctu atque miseriis mortem aerumnarum requiem, non cruciatum esse, eam cuncta mortalium mala dissolvere, ultra neque curae neque gaudio locum esse." (*BC* 51.20.) This is pure Epicureanism and represents the tone of his whole speech: an easy, cosmopolitan rationalism, divorced from any serious attachment to inherited institutions. Caesar minimizes, as much as possible under the circumstances, the danger offered by the conspiracy and argues for minimum punishment. He clearly is not concerned with the threat to the commonwealth, may have been part of that threat now, as he was to be later, and frames his speciously traditional appeals to commonwealth and history with the ideas of Hellenistic, even Epicurean, philosophizing, representative of the world in which he really lives, which is most certainly not the world of the *mos maiorum. Res* (reality) and *verum* (truth) are his themes, but his real definitions are not those he falsely plays upon for the delusion of his audience.

The full implications of Caesar's ideas are drawn out in Sallust's version of Cato's speech, which is everything Caesar's is not: "Longe mihi alia mens est." (*BC* 52.2.) Here now we see that union of Stoic thought and the Roman tradition by which the Old Believers adapted their belief to a more sophisticated view of the world and shaped the Greek thought with which they came in contact. Cato describes the conspirators as men "qui patriae, parentibus, aris atque focis suis bellum paravere." (*BC* 52.3.) This sets analysis squarely in the realm of traditional communal thought and locates judgment along the standard of *pietas, religio, fides,* and the *pax deorum.* Here is no argument from philosophic calm or an unrooted rationalism but direct invocation of the world of the Fathers. Sallust makes Cato expose Caesar's coy suggestion of mercy and then denounce his rhetorical and intellectual sharp practice: "Hic mihi quisquam mansuetudinem et misericordiam nominat. Iam pridem equidem nos vera vocabula rerum amisimus. Quia bona aliena largiri liberalitas, malarum rerum audacia fortitudo vocatur, eo res publica in extremo sita est." (*BC* 52.11.) This summarizes the crisis of the age. Words are floating free, divorced from the values and institutions to which they were attached. This Thucydidean theme had a great fashion in the Late Republic, and we shall see its variation in Catullus and Lucretius.

Caesarian smoothness comes under attack again (at 52.13), when Cato describes his discourse on life and death: "Bene et composite C. Caesar paulo ante in hoc ordine de vita et morte disseruit, credo falsa existumans ea quae de inferis memorantur, diverse itinere malos a bonis loca taetra, inculta, foeda, atque formidulosa habere." All the secrets of Caesar's speech stand forth in this contrast with the inherited belief: his twisting and uprooting of words, his rationalism, his subtlety of suggestion, his lack of feeling about traditional patterns, and his willingness at least to use Epicurean arguments to diminish the punishment of the enemies of ancient order.

In the two speeches Sallust gives us, he brings Caesar and Cato into opposition on the specific points of what *res* (reality) demands of our assumptions about things, the existence of the underworld, what is *verum* and what *falsum*, the employment of words, what constitutes a threat to *res publica*, and what the response should be to conspiracy against social life. They are in nearly complete disagreement because they live in two different worlds of thought. Yet, they appeal to the same history of the same *res publica*, use the same categories of rhetorical argument, and appeal by means of the same vocabulary to the same apparent values. The fact that their values are so different and so much of their apparent argument the same is a paradigm of the crisis. Viewing this difficulty from the perspective of an alien language, it is hard enough to sort out all the complexities of the intellectual confusion presented. Trying to clarify matters from inside the structure of Latin itself led to virtual impasse.

Caesar and his career represent the extreme point of the disaster of Republican ideas, because here value, motive, action, and language were farthest removed from one another, and appearances were most at odds with reality. Caesar used language not to express the inherited perceptions or to expand those perceptions under the pressure of novel experience or even to refute those perceptions by redefining the words and leading a new pattern of life. Rather, his career was conducted ostensibly on communal lines, his language was Republican and oligarchic, but his motives and goals were at odds with the inheritance, and his own views rejected the inherited system of procedure, categories, and purposes. The discord of seeming and being, when the old formulas and expressions were used to divert attention from reality and create convenient appearances, brings into doubt even the belief that there can be such a thing as truth, that there is anything more than appearance. Power becomes the only reality and appearance of truth its tool. Caesar himself embodies additional contradiction by accepting Epicurean principles as far as they rendered meaningless any institutions obstructive to his purpose and abandoning those principles at the point where they themselves became obstructions. Acceptance of Epicurean postulates as the foundation for an un-Epicurean pattern of life was not uncommon for the politicians of this age. It is similar to the use of Republican language to disguise un-Republican aims and an ultimately un-Republican pattern of behavior, but it throws into confusion the new Hellenism along with the old Republicanism. This, too, was common in the age, and both practices illustrate the impasse to which matters had come. The utility of language for conveying ideas and truth, the very possibility of having tests of truth amid such confusion of idea, was called into question. It is from this impasse that Catullus, Cicero, and Lucretius sought to rescue Latin.

5. *Catullus*

Catullus agreed with Caesar that the inherited system was corrupt and meaningless. Like Caesar, he rejected the *mos maiorum* as the foundation of action and value. Unlike Caesar, he admitted this and sought a new pattern of life, new sources of thought, and a means for reforming the inherited terms to express his account of life. Like Epicurus, Catullus viewed civil institutions as hopelessly corrupt and empty of significance. Like Epicurus, he declined to participate in public life. Unlike Epicurus, he did not reject the value of passion and of art. Unlike Epicurus, he did not find his source of knowledge and value in philosophy and the philosophical life.

Catullus poses the intellectual problem of the times in Poem 51. Beginning with a variation on a famous ode of Sappho, he records the reaction of personal feeling and resultant emotional disarray at the sight of his beloved. Extreme feeling and confusion arise because of the value placed upon the object of love and the act of love itself, which value he expresses by equating association with the beloved and the life of the gods, suggesting even that this association makes one superior to that life. This view is both un-Epicurean and un-Roman. Catullus implies the uncivic character of his declaration by the insertion of "si fas est" at the point where he suggests the superiority of love satisfied to divinity. This is not in Sappho, having nothing to do with the point of her poem, and is specifically Roman. Of course, this view of things is not *fas*. The gods of both Greece and Rome knew how to deal with those who thought themselves their betters, as Marsyas, Niobe, Pentheus, and Arachne discovered, and rewarded those who religiously served the common interest in their human capacity, as the great legends of the heroes of Rome taught. Inserting "si fas est" puts the poem in a Roman context and poses the problem of the conflict between civic and personal values. It forecasts Catullus' close with a strophe of his own composition as verses 13-16.

This closing strophe presents the reaction of the civic tradition. It criticizes the lover's state of emotional helplessness as the product of *otium*, which had led him to locate value in his own feelings and to distort reality to the degree that he could so misconceive the value of passion and divine life. Were he to engage in the search for civic honor, the proper pattern of life and the true location of worth outside the person in impersonal service, and were he to respect the gods in the traditional way, he would not find himself in this condition. The poem then closes with a homily from history and Hellenistic culture to reenforce the Roman ethical point.

Catullus does not resolve this clash of civic and neoteric value, but he raises the fundamental issue of the crisis, the implications of which he draws out in the rest of his poetry. He has found an uncivic source of worthiness, whose novelty and power he suggests by "si fas est" and the implied conflict with *religio* and *pietas*. He demonstrates how much his suggestion swerves from the dictates of *mos maiorum* by showing in the final strophe that the pattern of life and purpose described in the first three comes under the inherited category of *otium*, doing nothing. He will then in other poems explore the comparative worth of the old and the new categories, to reform the account of reality and relocate the standard of truth, investing his *otium* with a reformed *dignitas*. This will bring him into direct conflict with Cicero, whose role in the crisis will be described below.

Catullus portrays his new world in Poem 50, which he set before the Sapphic variation in his final ordering of his *libellus*, by placing *otiosi* in the first verse and associating the adjective with the world of art and artistic friendship founded on shared poetic and personal style and goals. Unlike Caesar, Catullus, once he has rejected the civic heritage, searches for a new standard of knowledge and truth, rather than abandoning the notions of truth and worth altogether.

The rest of Catullus' poems flow from his belief that the old terms for reality and standards of truth are valid only if filled with new content, content precisely the opposite of the old. Poem 5 rejects the authority of the *senes* and their censorship based on their *severitas* and supplants it and the ethic of *negotium* (satirized in the mock accounting list of kisses, where the point is to confuse the sum and not to give an accurate total) with the ethic of a purely private relationship between a man and a woman based on sincerity of personal feeling. This relationship he identifies with the substance and purpose of life itself. Such a point of view is civic nonsense, talk about empty things, things which are not part of reality in the world of *civitas*. That is why in Poem 1 Catullus admits his writing is *nugae* in the eyes of a Roman audience schooled in Republican virtue. *Nugae* in Poem 1 is parallel to *otium* in Poem 51. They both come from the ancestral standard of criticism. Only someone of daring equal to that of Catullus, like Cornelius (to whom the word *ausus* is applied), might understand, thus the fact that Cornelius finds some worth in his work, what we might call a new *dignitas*, is so important to Catullus and gives the reason for dedicating his *libellus* to this man of daring understanding.

In the ironic and witty Poem 45, he opposes the witty private relationship of a man and a woman to the *gloria* and *laus* gained by sharing in the extension of *imperium*. For Catullus, Acme and Septimius represent the reality of human life and in their urbanity and passion express the new values flowing from this more accurate perception of reality, as opposed to the empty words and false associations of the imperial adventurists. These two are the people truly blessed by the gods, a thought taking us back to the "si fas est" of Poem 51 and which we can contrast both with the civic ideal and the Epicurean notion of what constituted the godlike life for human beings.

The emptiness of the civic vocabulary and the inherent corruption of politics, particularly in its contemporary imperial guise, are Catullus' themes in Poem 29.[12] Political friendship is a sham, the corrupt imitation of real friendship. Political alliance and activity are imaged by corrupt sex and identified with corrupt enrichment at the expense of helpless peoples. Catullus again parodies the accounting list, here summing the wages of imperial crime and prodigality. He suggests the emptiness of public discourse, much of which had degenerated into brazenly manipulative partisan propaganda, in phrases like "cinaede Romule", "albulus columbus", "imperator unice", and "sinistra liberalitas", here offering his version of the theme of the separation between words and things. Financial and sexual corruption as the central images of modern politics reach their conclusion in the logic of modern life with the corruption of *pietas* itself by the familial alliance of Pompey and Caesar for corrupt and even anti-Republican gain referred to in "socer generque". This shows as clearly as anything in Catullus his conception of the inherent immorality of the old civic system. The very heart of that system, the family, is created by alliances made for gain, ultimately for

---

[12] See J. D. Minyard, "Critical Notes on Catullus 29", *CP* 76 (1971) 174-181.

gain that threatens the *res publica* based on it, and not as the expression of sincere feeling, in which by the time of Catullus it is possible to believe.

Catullus' treatment of politicians in his other poems makes sense in the context of his perception of the true foundation of values. That perception leads to the indifferent contempt of Caesar expressed in Poem 93 and the extrapolation of the image of sexual corruption linking him and Mamurra in Poem 57. Mamurra is reduced eventually to the pure, specific symbol of the truth about himself and his politics: the *mentula* of the epigrams. Memmius is pictured in the same terms. As Catullus mocks the pattern on which Pompey, Caesar, Crassus, Memmius, Piso, and Mamurra practice politics by identifying it with corrupt sex, theft, false friendship, and disgraceful marriage, so he reduces the Ciceronian practice to what he perceives as its essence: the corruption of language and indiscriminate friendship. Poem 49 parodies what Catullus would see as the self-centered pomposity and meaningless, indiscriminate superlatives of Ciceronian oratorical style, which eliminates language as an instrument of precise communication, and mocks the undiscriminating, meaningless friendships of the "optimus omnium patronus", so different from those of the discriminating "pessimus omnium poeta", who, on the same standard, would be, we may deduce, the real "optimus paucorum poeta" (compare Poem 95). The use of *optimus* here must hit at the language of Ciceronian political self-advertisement in the same way *liberalitas* and *imperator* make fun of the propaganda of Caesar and Pompey in Poem 29.

Catullus might have believed, or believed at one point, that the old pure world of *civitas*, as portrayed in Sallust's later myth of contemporary decline from a pure Republican past, represented true moral value and the paradigm of reality, but that this had been ruined by historical change and modern circumstance. Poems 61 and 62 on marriage and the end of Poem 64 on the decline of morals can be made to support this interpretation. Yet, his own account of reality, value, and truth, as it is expressed in the whole corpus of his composition, has nothing in common with the ancestral way. He not only makes fun of the mechanisms and lower purposes of imperial politics, and his own brief personal participation on the periphery of the same, but in Poem 28 he concludes with a rebuke of the inheritance and its modern form in the sarcastic "pete nobiles amicos": "that's what you get for seeking out politicians as 'friends'." It is better to see marriage, but marriage following on authentic feeling, as one institution of the patrimony that can be saved, but saved only if not used as a tool of civic ambition, and the fall from ancient grace in Poem 64 as a decline from heroic not civic worth, a time in the past, before the cities, when there was true marriage in the world and also *iustitia*. The gods left when civil conflict entered human life.

The foundation of Catullan values upon personal feeling and a style that dictates both a pattern of life and a pattern of art can be illustrated, for example, from such poems as 12, 14, 17, 22, 95, and 116. The qualities that make a good person are those shown by a good poem and include wit, irony, and urbanity, in addition to integrity and the faithfulness to personal feeling. Value in life is judged on the same standard as value in art. Suffenus may exhibit certain qualities in his personal manner that make him admirable in that sphere, but the superficiality of his qualities is shown by their absence in his art, which makes his poems false. Asinius Marrucinus' behavior lacks these qualities and can be condemned on that ground. The subject matter of worthwhile, i.e. true, poetry, should be the representation of a truthful and honest pattern of neoteric personal life.

In the process of setting out a personalistic account of the world, with a new standard of truth, Catullus, rather than creating new terms, redefines the old categories. This presents special problems for understanding him, problems which would have been even greater for his Roman audience, in much the same way it would have been difficult to understand precisely what Caesar was talking about. But the context in which he places the traditional terms makes his meaning clear to close reading. The best single example of this technique of redefinition is Poem 76, which is unintelligible if we read it by applying their old social meanings to the inherited words which appear in it: *benefacta, pius, sancta fides, foedus, salus, purus, pudicus, pietas.* What have all these to do with *amor* of the kind Catullus has exhibited and is talking about in this poem, except to condemn it and the man who has devoted himself to it at the expense of the world they refer to? Catullus is, however, claiming that his life has exemplified these values and lays claim specifically to *pietas*, on the basis of which he appeals to the gods for their favor. Everything he portrays himself as doing and defending in the rest of his poems can only be construed as an affront to civic *pietas*. Catullus knew this. Every schoolboy at Rome knew it. What then can he have meant?

Meaning can be given to Poem 76, on the assumption that Catullus is not simply trying to fool and confuse his audience, only by understanding the new definitions he gives the traditional language, the new world in which he has caused them to live. They are stripped of their social and civic reference and reapplied in a personal context, in which the test of truthfulness is not public action but authenticity of personal feeling as the motivation for the establishment of private, non-civic relationships. It is on these lines that *pietas* and the rest of the civic vocabulary in Poem 76 is to be interpreted (as well as "sanctae foedus amicitiae" in Poem 109). Catullus has not engaged in politics, and he is not speaking of

Republican values. His concern is his private relations, in this case with a married woman while her husband was still alive. The *fides* of this *foedus amicitiae* in their own *res privata* was located in personal feeling, in defiance of civil commitment. The *benefacta* were acts of love. The *salus* to which he refers is entirely private and personal, his inner emotional welfare and its physical consequences (as the metaphor of disease shows). His *pietas* was his truthfulness to his relationship with Lesbia, truthfulness to the warrant or *fides* of his feelings. This is what makes the Catullan use of the old words different from Caesar's. The poet's use of *pietas* and *fides* is not comparable to Caesar's assertion of *dignitas*, because Catullus has placed the words in an entirely new setting and given them a new anchor in the actual events of life. Caesar pretends to use the old word in the old context as the allegation of ancient right and value, but he is lying. He is using the word in a way the old context and ancient right does not allow. He is deliberately making nonsense of the term by employing it as the veil of new action not as the indication of a new kind of worth he has discovered in the world.

Catullus, however, creates a new reference of feeling for these words. Lesbia and her husband, however much married, were not joined in a union ratified by feeling. Therefore, the marriage was not real but an imitation. Respecting it would entail repudiation of the new *fides*, not its realization. Catullus' own feeling for Lesbia was genuine, therefore the foundation of a real *foedus amicitiae* because sanctified by true *fides*, not like the false *amicitiae* of public life. As it turned out, of course, Lesbia's declaration of sincere feeling was a sham. She had no *fides* because she had no feeling, and Catullus concentrates in a number of epigrams on the exploration of the gap between reality and her words.[13]

---

[13] On the whole question of Catullus' political vocabulary, see D. O. Ross, Jr., *Style and Tradition in Catullus* (Cambridge, Mass. 1969), especially 80-95. He isolates precisely the intellectual point of Poem 76 (89): "The most difficult question concerning c.76 is one that does not seem to have bothered any critic: what do the first five lines have to do with the sixth?" It may be doubted, however, if Ross exploits his insight fully. His phrase "vocabulary of political alliance" should be replaced by something like "language of civic association". Catullus' civic metaphor for his love constitutes ethical and intellectual revolution. Criticism of Ross' method in Minyard, *CJ* 69 (1973-1974) 88-91, and D. T. Benedickston, "Vocabulary Analysis and the Generic Classification of Literature", *Phoenix* 31 (1977) 341-348. Another account of Poem 76 is C. Rubino, "The Erotic World of Catullus", *CW* 68 (1974-1975) 289-298. There is much in Rubino's interpretation that is suggestive and can ultimately be integrated with the present discussion, especially the remarks on the entrapment of Catullus within the oligarchic intellectual system (293), as these show the oligarchic structure of Roman thought and the closeness of the intellectual class. But, on the whole, Rubino's position seems to me, *mutatis mutandis* for the modern analytical categories, a paradigm of what will have been the contemporary Roman reaction to Catullus among the Old Believers, to wit: "it is precisely the use of ... [legal and religious] terminology that makes Poem 76 and the entire complex of poems related to it

In Catullus, civic institutions, patterns, and goals are empty of content. They are the imitation of reality, an excuse or pretext for corruption, and so utterly lack *fides*. In a Roman setting, the poems of Catullus represent the extreme personalization of notions of truth, reality, and value. The person replaces the *res publica* in the shape of the *civitas* as the source of knowledge about reality and the location of the standard of truth. Personal feeling is the ground of our apprehension of the real-world and the measure of the worth of our experience.

In Catullus' rejection of the civic inheritance and the location of value in private life and personal feeling, there is an obvious overlap with Epicurean doctrine, hence the inclination to associate Catullus with contemporary Epicureanism, or Lucretius with contemporary neotericism. It is clear that Catullus emerges from the same historical circumstances that produced the popularity of Epicureanism in the Late Republic and that his poetry reflects the same crisis of ideas. We can see a similarity between some of his themes and perspectives and those of the Epicurean poets Lucretius and Philodemus.[14] But his notion of the value of passion is not Epicurean. Epicurus had established universally valid categories for the analysis of experience, test of truth, and control of the emotions. The ultimate test of truth and value was a public and testable process of reasoning from the phenomena of experience available to all persons equally on the same grounds. The feeling about these phenomena of each person had nothing to do with their status, evaluation, or interpretation.

Epicureanism also provided tests for the estimation of personal feeling, rejecting some feelings and advocating the moderation of all, but for Catullus there could be no question of the worth of sincere feeling, because this was the source of truth and the proper motivation of action. If, in his view, activity were controlled by convention alone, by external pressure, then it was only the imitation of experience, a false version of life. *Fides*, if it referred to an external warrant in behavior such that all the external forms were preserved regardless of what each party felt, was empty of content and the name of a corruption. If it referred to authentic feeling of faithfulness and loyalty, based on an emotional attraction and

---

mad" (291) and "the erotic world of Catullus thus turns out to be a deranged world, for darkness and madness exist at its very center, at its beginning, and at its end" (298). Jerome, perhaps reflecting a contemporary tale, says Lucretius went crazy too. In a linguistic sense, both poets—coupled by Nepos, who would have understood them both, in his life of Atticus—did.

[14] See L. Ferrero, *Poetica nuova in Lucrezio* (Firenze 1949); C. L. Neudling, "Epicureanism and the 'New Poets' ", *TAPA* 80 (1949) 429-430; J. I. M. Tait, *Philodemus' Influence on the Latin Poets* (Diss. Bryn Mawr 1941); E. J. Kenney, "Doctus Lucretius", *Mn* 23 (1970) 366-392.

harmony (the new *amicitia*), then it named a reality and not a deceptive manipulation. The same was true of *pietas*.

For Catullus, as not for Caesar, the old words retained utility, but only if they were removed from the social sphere in which they had originated and transferred to a realm not recognized in the *mos maiorum*: the interior life of feeling and personal relations. By what amounts to metaphysical metaphor, Catullus made a leap into the new realm: through the creation of a personal language of reference out of the material of the inherited social language to image an entirely new world of value.

6. *Cicero*

It is tempting to characterize Cicero's political and intellectual careers in passive terms and call him the anachronistic exemplar of a tradition he had not the political power or intellectual creativity to afford to recognize as dead. As a man of ideas he may seem a simple tourist of the various Greek philosophical systems, out of which he churned up a vulgarizing eclecticism. As a political thinker, he will have employed old words in old ways, devising nothing new in the service of his own uninventive ambition.

Such an interpretation would mistake Cicero's role in the crisis. His goal was the demonstration that not only could the *mos maiorum* accomodate Greek thought but that it could arbitrate between the competing Greek philosophical systems. His position was that the Roman categories, when properly understood, were flexible and potentially rich enough to comprehend the wider knowledge consequent upon Roman expansion into the Hellenistic world, and these categories and their concomitant values could provide a standard of truth for testing the validity of Greek assertion. Those Greek observations, arguments, and systems which were compatible, wholly or partially, with the ancestral framework and could be used to give it greater sophistication, subtlety, profundity, and universality, and could therefore be used to support the values of the ancient citizenry, were true. Those unable to serve this end, that in effect attacked the foundation of the old account, were false.

What might look like an easy-going eclecticism is actually evidence of a firm intellectual unity of conception and purpose. Stoicism, at least in its later forms, was particularly useful to the *mos maiorum*. Whatever might be said of the Old Stoa, it at least contained the seeds which allowed it eventually to enhance the intellectual content of *civitas*. The only system completely alien was Epicureanism. Here was the true, the clear, the total enemy, without any potentiality for reconciliation with the inherited form of the *res publica*, because it involved radical and necessary rejection of the culture of civic community. The seriousness of this threat to the Republican idea Cicero recognized, but in his eyes it was not *civitas* that was therefore on trial, with the obligation of justifying itself on the standard of an alien system. Its difficulties were the result of identifiable historical processes, not viciousness inherent in the old order itself, and could be cured by taking those processes into consideration.[15]

The clearest illustration of Cicero's position for the purposes of this essay comes from a treatise written near to the time of the deaths of Catullus and Lucretius, and therefore of the final form of their work: the *De Re Publica*. This has as its direct subject the worth of the *mos maiorum* and its continuing vitality in Classical intellectual life. The positions adopted in all his other writings flow from the foundations he describes in this work.

In the introduction to the dialogue, Cicero speaks of the contemporary reluctance to participate in politics (*versari in re publica*), particularly on the part of many adherents of philosophy, and his need to confute those who reject political activity and values before he can even enter upon a discussion of political philosophy. To the views of these philosophers, he opposes the civic criterion of value: "Nec vero habere virtutem satis est quasi artem aliquem nisi utare; etsi ars quidem cum ea non utare scientia tamen ipsa teneri potest, virtus in usu sui tota posita est; usus autem eius est maximus civitatis gubernatio, et earum ipsarum rerum quas isti in angulis personant, reapse non oratione perfectio." (*De Re Publica* 1.2.) Cicero preserves the traditional meaning of *virtus* as a pattern of action, not a potential or inner quality. It exists entirely (*tota*) in its employment in the social sphere. This is explicit denial of the possibility of a purely philosophical or intellectual *virtus*. This *virtus* in its best state retains its civic form, but the degree of change which has taken place in the world, and Cicero's recognition of the change, is indicated by his statement that the *maximus usus virtutis* resides in the *gubernatio civitatis*. The activity originally contained in the set is real and remains its foremost member, but there are now other activities therein, able to be included because they meet the test of the original item. This attitude is characteristic of the Ciceronian position and sets him apart from Caesar and Catullus. The set called *virtus* is not empty, nor has its content been revolutionized.

In the sentences immediately following the text quoted, Cicero brings together the entire structure of the categories of the *mos maiorum*, insisting on their historical social origin and defending this social experience as authentic knowledge, the origin of philosophical wisdom itself, and thus,

---

[15] See C. N. Cochrane (above, note 7) 37-60, for another discussion of Cicero's intellectual seriousness and positive cultural contributions in the context of Late Republican crisis.

of course, the ultimate test of the wisdom of the philosophers: "Nihil enim dicitur a philosophis, quod quidem recte honesteque dicatur, quod [non] ab iis partum confirmatum sit, a quibus civitatibus iura descripta sunt. unde enim pietas, aut a quibus religio? unde ius aut gentium aut hoc ipsum civile quod dicitur? unde iustitia fides aequitas? unde pudor continentia fuga turpi[tu]dinis adpetentia laudis et honestatis? unde in laboribus et periculis fortitudo? nempe ab iis qui haec disciplinis informata alia moribus confirmarunt, sanxerunt autem alia legibus." (*De Re Publica* 1.2.) The claim made here makes no sense if, just oppositely from Catullus, the original social and civic meaning of these words was not still uppermost in Cicero's mind and unless he judged the values expressed in the various philosophical systems on the standard of their social utility, that is, their conformity to civic wisdom. The centrality in his imagination of the *mos maiorum* as the source of true knowledge is summarized in his concluding traditionally Roman conception of the foundation of *leges* in *mores*.

The form itself of the *De Re Publica* is an attempt not only to validate the basis of traditional knowledge but also to assert the necessarily traditional foundation of real knowledge. Not only does Cicero claim repeatedly to find the source of truth and knowledge in the history of *res publica Romana*, that the Romans have discovered in their history all that the Greek speculative thinkers have discovered and validated these discoveries by the test of experience, but he places the conversation itself in the past, among a group of the *maiores*, and claims the report of this conversation was transmitted to him orally by someone who was a young man at the time of the dialogue but *maior* to Cicero, who was himself a young man when he heard it. Indeed Scipio Minor says he is simply reporting the wisdom he has learned from Cato Maior. This is the structure of the dialogue's plot. So, Cicero's concession to Greek rationalism by writing political philosophy under the influence of Greek theory,[16] taking time from the *maximus usus virtutis* for this compatible but derivative *minor usus*, which will have value because it defends, articulates, and so serves the *maximus usus*, is contained within, restrained by, the old mode of acquiring and testing knowledge. The structure of the *De Re Publica* thereby itself becomes the physical form of its notion of how knowledge is acquired and validated, through social experience, wherin is located its *fides*, and is transmitted from one generation to the next in the instruction of the young by the old. We may note, also, that the conversation Cicero

---

[16] On the Greek background of the *De Re Publica* and for a full discussion of the philosophical framework, see G. H. Sabine and S. B. Smith (trans.), *On the Commonwealth: Marcus Tullius Cicero* (1929; repr. Library of Liberal Arts).

purports to have had with Publius Rutilius Rufus took place in Smyrna, during his youthful study in the schools of Hellas, so he incorporates the new wider setting of civic ideas by the imperial and Hellenistic color he gives the treatise, imaging the changed character of the world to which the civic categories must be applied.

In Book 2, Cicero openly contrasts the sources of philosophical and social knowledge. In his claim to be handing down the views of Cato the Elder, Scipio the Younger says that Cato said the Roman Republic excelled other commonwealths *because* it had no single lawgiver, denigrating thereby a central feature of Hellenic culture. He goes on: "...nostra autem res publica non unius esset ingenio sed multorum, nec una hominis vita sed aliquot constituta saeculis et aetatibus. nam neque ullum ingenium tantum extitisse dicebat, ut quem res nulla fugeret quisquam aliquando fuisset, neque cuncta ingenia conlata in unum tantum posse uno tempore providere, ut omnia complecterentur sine rerum usu ac vetustate. quam ob rem, ut ille solebat, ita nunc mea repetet oratio populi Romani originem; libenter enim etiam verbo utor Catonis. facilius autem quod est propositum consequar, si nostram rem publicam vobis et nascentem et crescentem et adultam et iam firmam atque robustam ostendero, quam si mihi aliquam, ut apud Platonem Socrates, ipse finxero." (*De Re Publica* 2.2-3.) Cicero is not purporting here to reject Greek ideas but Greek method, not the truth of what the philosophers say, but their way of knowing whether what they say is true or not. His point, above all else, is that real knowledge cannot be the product of the private insight of one man alone, since the test must always be historical and social, and in looking for truth we must not make up things in our heads, like Socrates in Plato, but share in public thought. We must look outside ourselves for the origin and validation of ideas, conforming our inward minds to the outward forms of society. There is located the *fides* of ideas, the only *fides* of knowledge, not in the logic of individual thinking.[17]

---

[17] Compare Cicero's use of rhetoric as a mode of thought and instrument of analysis in his self-debate over whether to adhere to Caesar or Pompey (*Ad Att.* 9.4). He wrote speeches in both Greek and Latin, showing his awareness of the relation between language and thought, and asked Atticus (*Ad Att.* 8.11, repeated 8.12.6) to send him the περὶ Ὁμονοίας of Demetrius of Magnesia to help him in his deliberation. This is good evidence for the linguistic sophistication of the age, the seriousness of rhetoric as a vehicle of reasoning, and the contemporary consciousness of the link between language and idea. On these points, see also M. P. O. Morford, "Ancient and Modern in Cicero's Poetry", *CP* 62 (1967) 112-116, for more evidence of Cicero's linguistic experience, his pride in Latin, his Romanism, and the grounds on which his whole career, artistic as well as political and intellectual, represents a rejection of the values Catullus came to represent. Also compare Starr (above, note 7) 19-30, on the contrast between Caesarism and Ciceronianism. See Ch. Wirszubski, "Cicero's *Cum Dignitate Otium*: a Reconsideration", *JRS* 44

7. Lucretius

It is from this context of intellectual conflict that the *De Rerum Natura* of Lucretius takes its origin and gains its form. Whatever the problems presented by the relationship of Lucretius and his poem to the history of Epicureanism and the Epicurean communities of contemporary Italy, and there are many, there is no difficulty in relating them to the cultural environment of Late Republican Rome.[18]

As an event in the history of technical philosophy, it takes long, involved, and special argument to consider the *De Rerum Natura* anything but a sport. As a philosophical treatise, it is unlike anything in the tradition after the discovery of the dialectic. It is also specifically unlike what Epicurus declared to be the form of discourse proper to philosophy, unlike anything we know, directly or indirectly, about the Epicurean treatises of the First Century B.C. in Greek or Latin. On the basis of a knowledge of Epicureanism before Lucretius and of Epicureanism in contemporary Italy outside Lucretius, it would have been difficult to predict or expect this poem. In this case, the gap between expectation and event, between the previous history of Epicureanism and this event in Epicurean history, is very great, if, indeed, the facts allow us to consider this poem an event in Epicurean history. Observers of Epicureanism would not only not have expected the *De Rerum Natura*, they would confidently have predicted the impossibility of authentic

---

(1954) 1-13, for an account of Cicero's concern with this important theme of the age, to which Poems 50 and 51 of Catullus, and indeed the whole of the Catullan corpus, must be compared—e.g., "visum duxerat e foro otiosum" (10.2), a highly suggestive juxtaposition. The pressures of the times operated not only on *virtus* but on the whole of inherited thought and made it especially needful to find a kind of *dignitas* (civil or uncivil) for *otium*. The solutions of Catullus and Cicero were quite different. Cicero's letter to Trebatius on the latter's conversion to Epicureanism (*Ad Fam.* 7.12) contains an explicit statement of Cicero's perception of the relation of Epicureanism to civic life, e.g.: "Sed quonam modo ius civile defendes, cum omnia tua causa facias, non civium?" (7.12.2.) This is clear proof of whom specifically he had in mind at the beginning of the *De Re Publica*. Compare also Wirszubski's "*Audaces*: A Study in Political Phraseology", *JRS* 51 (1961) 12-22, for the contemporary prominence of this word, Cicero's usage, and another contrast with Catullus, as in the poet's application of *ausus es* to Cornelius in Poem 1. This strengthens the implications of Poem 1 and the present argument about Catullus' point of view, including its anti-traditional and anti-Ciceronian character.

[18] Two recent surveys of the issues in Lucretian studies, with bibliography of major works attached, are M. F. Smith, *Lucretius: De Rerum Natura* (Cambridge, Mass. 1975) ix-lx and E. J. Kenney, *Lucretius* (Oxford 1977). On Lucretius and poetry, see: E. E. Sikes, *Lucretius: Poet and Philosopher* (Cambridge 1931); J. H. Waszink, *Lucretius and Poetry* (Amsterdam 1954); P. H. Schrijvers, *Horror ac Divina Voluptas* (Amsterdam 1970), with review by E. J. Kenney, *CR* 22 (1972) 348-351; and J. D. Minyard, *Mode and Value in the De Rerum Natura: A Study in Lucretius's Metrical Language* (Wiesbaden 1978), 1-7 and 87-102. On Lucretius and Epicureanism, see P. Boyancé, *Lucrèce et l'épicurisme* (Paris 1963) and, now, D. Clay, *Lucretius and Epicurus* (Ithaca 1983).

Epicureanism taking such a turn. Of all the events likely to have been caused by Epicureanism, this one was likely to so small a degree that it could easily have been thought impossible. Of course Philodemus wrote poetry. But his poetry was like that of Catullus, like the tradition of Hellenistic epigram from which the poetry of Catullus took its start. When he came to write philosophy, he wrote it the way Epicurus said it should be written.

It is difficult to see how Lucretius cannot be thought isolated from the philosophical community of his time. Nothing in the form or method of his work suggests he was a schoolman or even a disciple of the schoolmen of the Garden or its colonies in any technical or official sense. We can point to no evidence that Lucretian innovations in doctrine, should any be found, would have been recognized as valid by the School. That is, while he clearly claims to be a follower of Epicurus, is this anything more than his claim? An Epicurean in the broad, cultural sense he surely was, but can we call him, in terms of the historical realities, an Epicurean in the narrow sense, i.e. an officially and publicly recognized, not to say authorized, exponent of doctrine?[19]

In the framework of the literary and intellectual history of Rome, the *De Rerum Natura* presents no such gap between expectation and actuality.

---

[19] See below, note 34, for some studies relevant to this question, and also the discussion in section 8, "The Consequences of Crisis", for observations on the illusion of Lucretius' cultural isolation. The issue of Lucretius' relation to his times, "The idea of Lucretius as a lone hand" (as Kenney puts it on page 6 of his *Lucretius*), is twofold, philosophical and literary. Isolation in one sphere does not imply isolation in another. Kenney's summary (*Lucretius* 7) is to the point: "The most important and the most reliable inferences that can properly be made from the *D.R.N.* are of a literary order. Mention has been made of the wide culture pervading the poem. Lucretius, however, was not only well read, observant, and intelligent. He was more especially a professional poet, professional in the sense that he wrote as one dedicated to the futherance of an ancient poetic tradition, the didactic *epos*; and his poem belongs to the mainstream of ancient literary development." This essay is an attempt to provide additional support for this point of view, but we should not allow such wholly correct observations to obscure the fact that Lucretius' poem was the most original poetic document in the history of the Classical literatures. Poetry was no longer the medium for real philosophy and was not supposed ever to be the medium for Epicureanism: no one had written a poem about a philosophical system which forbade the philosophical use of poetry. And we should remember that Epicureanism was a living system with a school. This is not true of the ancient and dead philosophy, dead as a still-creative independent system, and one which never had a school, of Empedocles. Whatever Sallustius did, he was not facing the issues Lucretius faced. Lucretius did not intend simply to give a poetic reproduction or literary turn to a philosophical or scientific topic. He intended to set literature on a new path. This is not, however, the kind of originality suggested by D. Clay, "*De Rerum Natura*: Greek Physis and Epicurean Physiologia (Lucretius 1.1-148)", *TAPA* 100 (1969) 31-47, although he well observes (32) the distinction between Lucretius' poem and Ennius' *Epicharmus*, Cicero's *Aratea*, and Sallustius' *Empedoclea*. See now D. Clay, *Lucretius and Epicurus* (above, note 18) 82-110. See also Kenney's *Lucretius: De Rerum Natura Book III* (Cambridge 1971) for many detailed observations on the poem's literary character.

Lucretius and his poem look like perfectly logical consequences of the general set of circumstances, the tendencies, pressures, and interests, of the culture of the Late Republic. It is possible to point to many previous events leading in its direction, as well as many contemporary events in harmony with it. His poem reflects all the major literary fashions and trends of the age. If we were to judge the nature of contemporary philosophy from Lucretius' poem, we should have a very odd idea of what it was like. But it is easy to see what the rest of Late Republican literature was like from the De Rerum Natura. If we were allowed to have the work of one author only from this period as evidence of its literature, it would be difficult to find an example more comprehensively indicative.

Indeed, the De Rerum Natura makes no claim to be an event in the history of philosophy. It does not declare that it contributes to the development of philosophical method or knowledge but to Roman moral understanding and cultural life. It attempts to apply a philosophical system to the realm of Roman social behavior. This is, of course, what Epicurus did in a Greek context, but after he had developed method and knowledge, created a system and a school, with followers and philosophical argument, confuting his technical opponents as well as making positive technical contributions. Lucretius is a literate and literary Roman who sees, as a man of culture, observer of history, and an ambitious poet, the historical, social, moral, and poetic utility of this accomplishment, not to say the literary main chance. The context in which he places his poem is Roman, oligarchic, and literary, not Greek, scholastic, and philosophical.

It is important to set the proper frame in which to interpret the work of Lucretius. Without a frame of reference, it is not possible accurately to perceive an event, let alone judge its causes, consequences, and significance. Without agreement on the world of a work, it is not even possible for readers to discuss it, because divergence in the ground of expectation, evaluation, and interpretation will produce a series of monologues, even soliloquies, masquerading as dialogue. The history of Roman literature and the intellectual crisis of the Late Republic explain the form and content of the De Rerum Natura, and the relationship between its form and content: why this content was chosen and then put in, of all things, this form. Within this frame, the poem is perfectly intelligible. It is hardly intelligible as a coherent whole as a philosophical treatise at this point in the history of philosophical discourse and method.[20]

---

[20] There are more studies than there used to be attempting to relate Lucretius to his age and to Roman culture. Important among these are: E. J. Kenney, "Doctus Lucretius", Mn 23 (1970) 366-392; P. Grimal, "Le Poème de Lucrèce en son Temps" in Entretiens Hardt XXIV (Genève 1978) 233-270 (which reaches some conclusions very different from

Its famous First Proem sets a Roman, historical, and civic context for
the *De Rerum Natura* by its allusions to contemporary strife and such
language as "Aeneadum" (1), "patriai tempore iniquo" (41), "com-
muni ... saluti" (43), "impia" (81), "civis" (91), "felix faustusque"
(100), "virtus" (140), and "amicitiae" (141), along with the address to
the oligarch Memmius and the criticism of the heritage of *religio* which
begins here and runs through the poem. The addition to these elements
of Greek philosophy ("Graius homo" at 66), Greek mythology (the story
of what happened at Aulis at 84-100), Greek literature (the association of
Ennius, Helicon, and Homer at 117-126), and the universal descriptions
and prescriptions offered as remedies for human ills, unrooted as they are
in the particular experience of any specific people as an historical entity,
imparts a radically cosmopolitan ambience which both gives the poem a
dual origin and reveals its uncivil point. The *De Rerum Natura* is made to
emerge from the ruin of civil order as the non-civic remedy for the errors
and evil inherent in that order as the seeds of its own destruction.

The first sixty-one verses of the proem contrast two ways of dealing
with the world, that of *civitas* and that of, as we later learn, Epicurus. The
first verse gives us *voluptas* and verse 43 *communis salus*, suggesting two opposing aims of life, at least as the phrase *communis salus* is understood in
its civic context. Although Lucretius prays for peace because he cannot
set about his task with an even temper amid such civil strife and Memmius cannot devote himself to instruction because he cannot desert the
cause of the welfare of the community, in fact, the point of the poem will
be precisely to argue the preservation of an even temper amid all circumstance, based on *vera ratio rerum*, and that Memmius should desert the
communis salus as traditionally understood because the category is empty
of intellectual and moral value. Indeed devotion to *communis salus* has led
to the very crisis at which Rome now finds itself. What Lucretius will be
doing in the poem to come will be instructing Memmius in what amounts
to a conception of true *salus*.

The opening section of the First Proem is artful in all senses, not exactly misleading the reader, in terms of his ultimate understanding, but using words and expressions he thinks he understands already in order to
get him to follow the new path Lucretius is tracing. The end of this will be
the creation of a different meaning for the opening of the poem in the eyes
of the reader. As a hint of this, Lucretius affords a brief vision of his goal

---

those of this essay about that relationship, particularly in regard to Caesar); see also,
A. K. Michels, "Lucretius, Clodius and Magna Mater" in *Mélanges ... offerts à J. Car-
copino* (Paris 1966) 675-679, on a specific point of contact beween the poem and contemporary life. The works of Farrington (above, note 8) also place Lucretius in his historical
setting.

in verses 44-49, designed to shock the reader into a confusion about the coherence of this assertion with the preceding hymn. The poem will move repeatedly by this method of contradiction and abrupt transition to force the reader into perception of a larger, and deeper, order in the poem and in the world than that of which he, on the basis of his *falsa ratio*, is presently aware.

Having prayed to a Venus which the Romans understand as a force in nature and history, alluded to Memmius' duty to *communis salus*, and then declared the material basis of reality and the absence of providence from the world, Lucretius leads his perhaps shaken but surely aroused reader through a devastation of the civic inheritance by striking at what he considers its core, the category named *religio*. After what the poet has just said about the indifferent gods, it is clear that *religio* must represent a false notion of reality, an empty set in terms of its claimed reference, and a terrible scandal in social life, since it is around this name that the inherited community was organized and on this basis that its history has been interpreted. For this poet, however, instead of referring to the principal line of interaction between humanity and divinity, along with its positive corollary *pietas*, and being thus central to the true understanding of reality and well-being (*salus*), it is a heavy oppression upon mankind.

The close connection between *religio* and *pietas* in the traditional account of reality, as opposite sides of the same coin and interdependent elements of a coherent intellectual structure, Lucretius recognizes in verse 81, where he acknowledges that his reader may think he is seducing him to impiety by his denunciation of *religio*. He could simply deny this potential allegation, but he does not. He could empty the category *pietas* of content and treat it with scorn too, but he does not do this either, even though, given the interdependence of *religio* and *pietas*, this is what we might have expected him to do. What he does do is to give us verse 83: "religio peperit scelerosa atque impia facta." This assertion, in the structure of traditional Latin, is madness. On the basis of the meaning of Latin words, it cannot be true. *Religio* is divorced from *pietas* and converted into its opposite: *religio* is *impia*. The point is even repeated, as the dictum of verse 101: "tantum religio potuit suadere malorum." It is the verses between 83 and 101, in which Lucretius performs the surgery of separating *pietas* from *religio*, that distil most clearly the method and purpose of the poem, as well as the poet's striking dialectical and poetic originality, power, and genius. The interpretation of this passage provides the key to Lucretius' procedure, aims, and relation to the Latin language.

The sacrifice of Iphigeneia (Iphianassa) by her father Agamemnon is part of the most famous and culturally important of the Greek mythic cycles. The Trojan legends embodied the core of Greek values, provided the content for the most famous works of Greek literature, and, in their Homeric form, were the center of Greek education. In picking a legend from this group, Lucretius strikes the heart of Classical literary, ethical, and political culture. He chooses a Greek story rather than an incident from Roman history because his aim is reformation of the literary tradition by provision of a new kind of epic and hero, replacing the *Iliad* as a source of knowledge and Achilles as a model with a philosophically sound epic and Epicurus as a model, much the way Plato sought to substitute for them the dialectic and Socrates and Virgil in the next generation will offer a world reshaped by Roman imperialism an epic of modern historical and philosophical content and Aeneas as the representative, imitable hero. Since Lucretius' target is the whole shape and content of civic culture in the Greco-Roman form it has now realized at Rome, the story of Iphigeneia has special pertinence. What better illustration of service to *communis salus* than the epic and tragic sacrifice of a daughter by her father for the common welfare at the direction of divinity in order to fight a war which will gain for its heroes greatest reknown and value? This tale from the center of civic literature will stir to life in any Roman mind all the grand categories: *religio, pietas, familia, communis salus, gloria, laus, virtus, pater, fides*.

In this story, the mythology, literature, and pattern of life of the civic tradition coalesce to play right into Lucretius' hands. They deliver themselves as evidence against themselves to show how the Epicurean philosophy can furnish the basis for a coherence between fact and values in literature and life and, by implication, for a new literature and ethic. The sacrifice of Iphianassa, in attonement and purification to remove the guilt incurred by violating what was *sacer* to a divinity, evokes the world of *pietas* (and its verb *pio*), an act of which is here enjoined to cleanse the *pater* and *rex* who has been stained by a violation of the prohibitions of *religio*. But *pietas* is also the foundation of the religion of the family and is thus the bond of obligation that gives separate form to each family. The passage flourishes conflict within the category *pietas*, between the *pietas* of *pater* and that of *rex*, as Lucretius hammers away at the relationship between Iphianassa and Agamemnon and the violation of the expectations arising from that relationship under the pressure of *religio*: "ante aras adstare parentem / sensit" (89-90), "patrio princeps donarat nomine regem" (94), and "parentis" (99). More than this, since the king's daughter was brought to Aulis on the pretext of marriage, *religio* makes mock of the very foundation of familial *pietas*, a mockery perpetrated by the abrogation of *fides*. The agents of the deception, in addition to the *rex*, denying his obligation as *pater*, are the "ductores delecti", the "prima virorum'', and the ''civis''. The princess is led to the altar supported ''virum manibus''. No Roman reading this passage could escape thinking of *nobiles*, *civitas*, and *virtus*. The purpose of this filthy bloodshed—and surely ''foede'' in 85 is meant to mock the meaning of *pio* and *pietas*—is described in the ancient civic formula of verse 100: ''exitus ut classi felix faustusque daretur.'' The civic classes and their purposes conspire in the name of *religio* to accomplish *impia facta*. The aim of civic life is a lie and the consequences of its ethic are its own condemnation.

The key words for which the *mos maiorum* asserted coherence and mutual justification (*religio*, *pietas*, *fides*, *pater*, *familia*, *civitas*, *virtus*) are set at odds with one another. Lucretius does not so much shred the inheritance in this passage as allow it to shred itself, by the simple device of citing one of its own self-justifying stories. What before were interdependent entities become inimical to each other, and the old structure collapses from its own inner contradictions. No strategy for demolishing the civic idea could have been more effective or have accomplished more of his goals than the one Lucretius chose. Rather than succumbing to the temptation of scornful denunciation of the view he opposes, he allows it to denounce itself. He accepts the story of Iphianassa and her father as true. Literature does not here tell a false tale but a true one about what happens when people have a false view of the world. Where the ancestral literature is false is in its assumptions about reality and in the conclusions about purpose and value it draws from the events it relates. This is a condition Lucretius seeks to rectify. Since the literature is part of the unified civic tradition, illustrating its self-contradiction and errors attacks the whole of the inheritance and launches the Lucretian enterprise of reshaping Roman life and the literary tradition on the standard of the true Epicurean account of reality. The poet's purpose is not philosophical innovation or instruction for its own sake, or instruction itself as the tool of reform. The innovations have been made already and the instruction is available elsewhere. If instruction itself were to be his instrument and philosophical reform his aim, the standard form of Epicurean discourse was a more efficient, direct, and unambiguous medium. His aim was to show the ramifications of doctrine for civic life and literary innovation by the creation of a new literature acceptable to modern knowledge founded on received doctrine to replace the old literature founded on a received and scientifically naive mythology. He begins his journey to both literary and civic ends by selecting a story from the literary handling of the mythological heritage that illustrates the self-induced fissures in the civic system of ideas.

In this passage, Lucretius achieves a positive as well as a negative result, for he begins the process of rearranging the Roman perception of reality by commencing the rearrangement of the Roman language for that reality. As an Epicurean, he could not accept *religio*, but he could accept *pietas*, if the role of the gods were properly defined. Indeed, he would want to accept a reformed understanding of *pietas*, because it was a category potentially important to Epicurean ethics as a support to its conception of the attitude of men toward the gods. So, he does not reject the name *pietas*. He divorces it from *religio* and saves the word for redefinition by condemning *religio* as its enemy.

Lucretius' procedure is exactly the opposite of Cicero's. Cicero applied the test of the civic system to Greek systems and accepted or rejected on that basis. Epicureanism failed this test, partly because it could not meet the requirements of both *religio* and *pietas*. Lucretius subjects *civitas* to the test of Epicureanism and accepts and rejects on that basis. This is a test which *pietas*, when properly instructed, can be made to pass and *religio* cannot. For Cicero, the *mos maiorum* has proven itself because the test of truth is the test of historical experience and is social. For Lucretius, Epicureanism has proven itself because the test of truth is sense perception interpreted by accurate science or rule (the canonic or *ratio*) and is private. The insights and observations of Epicureanism contain the warrant or credit (*fides*) of statements about the world. *Religio*, therefore, is a lie.

A neat tactic enables Lucretius to symbolize both his view of the origin of knowledge and the fact that he is holding Roman social traditionalism to the standard of Hellenic rationalism. In verse 66, he refers to Epicurus in his description of that philosopher's great service to man by his triumph over the gods, but he does not name him. He uses the phrase "Graius homo".[21] This sharpens the conflict between mankind and the gods of tradition, emphasizing the human sources of knowledge. It stresses the notion that the source of truth is individual, not societal. In this connection, Lucretius also suggests a new meaning, or at least a new application, for *virtus*, when, at verse 70, he makes Epicurus' rebellion

---

[21] L. Edelstein, "Primum Graius Homo (Lucretius 1.66)", *TAPA* 71 (1940) 78-90, does not believe Lucretius had Epicurus in mind here. His arguments seem to me far-fetched and based on a misreading of the poem, to wit (89): "Moreover, one should not overemphasize the importance of religion for Lucretius' thinking and consequently not overestimate the importance which the liberation from religious fears through Epicureanism has for the poet's mind." The entire present essay is an answer to this point of view. Edelstein's argument, however, rightly emphasizes the generality of the Lucretian phrase: that the poet at this point stresses the Greekness of the accomplishment, rather than the identity of the individual. Compare "Graiorum obscura reperta" at 1.136. On Lucretius as a *follower* of Epicurus, see D. J. Furley, "Lucretius the Epicurean", *Entretiens Hardt* XXIV (Genève 1978) 1-6. On the centrality of the struggle against religion to Epicurus, see Farrington, *Science and Politics* (above, note 8) 87-129, 148-159, and 172-216 (on Lucretius), and *The Faith of Epicurus* (above, note 8) 63-104.

against the heart of civil order (*religio*) flow from his *animi virtus*. This contradiction of the inherited social notion of *virtus*, and its separation from *religio*, lays the foundation for the new socially deracinated conception of *pietas* in the Iphianassa passage to follow. Again, we contrast Cicero, who denigrated the achievements of individual Greek law-givers and speculators, in comparison to the experience of *res publica Romana* over many generations.

If we think so often of the Ciceronian position in the First Proem, we are also reminded of Catullus in verse 79. Epicurus' insights have raised humanity to the level of the gods: "nos exaequat victoria caelo." This is the true source of supreme human happiness, that which can be called divine, not the celebration of a *triumphus* or victory in one of the great Greek games, let alone the association with the beloved of a faithful heart we find in Catullus' extrapolation of Sappho in Poem 51, whose perspective Catullus recalls in Poem 72, when he tells us that once upon a time Lesbia's story was that she preferred him to Jupiter.

We may recall both Cicero and Catullus at verse 141, in the phrase "suavis amicitiae". Not only can we think of the importance of *amicitia* as a civic pattern and Cicero's later handling of the topic in his *De Amicitia*, but we can compare Catullus' "sanctae foedus amicitiae" in Poem 109, an *amicitia* founded on passion and guaranteed by the *fides* or credit of personal feeling, and his concern with the nature of friendship in so many of his poems, particularly the contrast between personal and civil friendships.

The First Proem outlines the Lucretian revaluation of the Roman inheritance of knowledge, which will be worked out and justified in detail in the rest of the poem. It devastates *religio* and dispenses with *fama* as a source of knowing, because "fama deum" (68, and compare 5.1133-1135) is a lie whose defeat is secured by *mens*, *virtus animi*, and *vivida vis animi*, the private process of intellect that will supplant the social *mos maiorum* on the basis of a new source of *fides*. A new frame of reference is indicated for *pietas*, *virtus*, *victor* (75), and *victoria* (79), and possibly *salus* (43). The other side of this reshaping consists in the elevation of other old words to the status of fundamental categories of analysis: *voluptas*, *ratio*, and *res*. The principal subdivisions of the idea of *res* are named, here and later in Book 1: *primordia*, *semina*, and *corpora*, i.e. the constituents of *res* can be looked at from different points of view. After the proem, Lucretius adds *inane*, which with *res* will refer to the fundamental bifurcation of reality, the sum beyond which there is nothing real. The new *virtus*, insofar as it exists at all, is intellectual, and the new *pietas* recognizes the serene indifference of divinity. The new aim of life is *voluptas*, replacing or redefining *communis salus*. The source of knowledge will not be *fama* or social experience but sense perceptions (*naturae species*), which will be the new locus of *fides*, and the Epicurean or *vera ratio* of these sense percep- tions will replace the *mos maiorum* as the evaluation or account of, the calculation or judgment upon this knowledge. The true accounting or *ratio* will rely on the *fides* of activity in the physical not the social world. Social experience will no longer provide the key to understanding nature. Nature will explain the true character and status of social experience. The new order of relations finds a paradigm at 1.422-425:

> corpus enim per se communis dedicat esse
> sensus; cui nisi prima fides fundata valebit,
> haud erit occultis de rebus quo referentes
> confirmare animi quicquam ratione queamus.

Sensus, *res*, and *ratio* replace *civitas* and its *mos* as the world of *fides* and knowledge.

Whatever else Lucretius has in mind by way of Greek terms when he uses *ratio*, and when he contrasts *vera* and *falsa ratio*, he must be thinking at least of the canonic, which otherwise seems to find no direct reference in his poem. This interpretation will cohere best with the core of meaning in the Latin word (as distinguished from its various references or applica- tions) and cause its extensions of reference (e.g., "caeli rationes" at 5.1183) to fly distinctive Epicurean colors everywhere. Truthfulness of statements about reality and value will now be tested on the standard of *vera ratio*, because it is based ultimately on the perception of the world's own figures or bookkeeping, e.g. "caeli rationes". With the true method of accounting, it will be possible to add up the sum correctly and strike an accurate balance.[22]

---

[22] See C. Bailey, *Titi Lucreti Cari De Rerum Natura Libri Sex* (Oxford 1947) 1227-1229, in- troducing his comments on 4.379-468, the description of false inferences of the mind, which he says (1228), "goes right back to the foundation of the Epicurean metaphysic ex- pressed in the *Canonice*" and 1177, where he notes that much of 4.1-822 "is concerned with Epicurus' *Canonice*...." At 4.384-385, Lucretius states the relation of sense percep- tion to understanding: "hoc animi demum ratio discernere debet, / nec possunt oculi naturam noscere rerum." The use of *ratio* here ("animi ... ratio") is very important to the point of the present argument. See D. J. Furley, "Lucretius the Epicurean" (above, note 21) 8: "... the pre-Epicurean terror and darkness of mind must be dismissed by *naturae species ratioque...* —that is, by looking at nature *and interpreting it*." The close association of *species* and *ratio* in the Lucretian phrase, making of the expression a nearly undivided con- cept, finds its foundation in the Epicurean rooting of judgment and thought directly in sensation. See the account of the Epicurean canonic in J. M. Rist, *Epicurus: An Introduction* (Cambridge 1972) 14-40. The importance of this understanding of *ratio* for the topic at hand is indicated by Rist's remarks on 15: "Epicurean canonic, therefore, is an enquiry into the nature of the tools we possess for knowing the external world and an evaluation of the information with which these tools supply us. As such, it is in the first instance an in- vestigation of what the Greeks were accustomed to call the criterion of truth or the

The centrality to the *De Rerum Natura* of the revaluation of the linguistic categories of reality in order to achieve civic and literary ends is confirmed near the end of the First Proem by verses 136-145, where, after the passage about Homer, Ennius, and the transference of Greek literature to Italy, all three factors combine to lay the basis for the poem's goal of enlightenment (146-148). They establish a literary and civic purpose for the enlightenment, which will require categorical shifts.

> Nec me animi fallit Graiorum obscura reperta
> difficile inlustrare Latinis versibus esse,
> multa novis verbis praesertim cum sit agendum
> propter egestatem linguae et rerum novitatem;
> sed tua me virtus tamen et sperata voluptas
> suavis amicitiae quemvis efferre laborem
> suadet et inducit noctes vigilare serenas
> quaerentem dictis quibus et quo carmine demum
> clara tuae possim praepandere lumina menti,
> res quibus occultas penitus convisere possis.

The passage stresses the poetic mode of presentation and the poetic problem: "difficile inlustrare Latinis versibus", "laborem", and "dictis quibus *et quo carmine*". Lucretius' concern is the composition and employment of Latin verses, the choice of diction, and the choice of poetic form. This is encompassed within the larger linguistic difficulty: "multa novis verbis" and "propter egestatem linguae". Latin as it exists does not provide the terms, the categories, necessary to explain the true nature of reality. The other side of the coin is that the Latin of the *mos maiorum* does not give a true account of reality. So Lucretius ascribes his problem not only to the "Graiorum obscura reperta" but to its Roman novelty: "novis verbis" and "rerum novitatem".

Newness at Rome was a far stronger, far more ominous category than it can be in an age or society where it has taken the rank of a primordial value. The political connotations of "novis" and "novitatem" could not be avoided in a language in which *novus homo* and *novae res* and *novae tabellae* were terms of such power or in an age when conspiracy and revolution were the air of political life. We might also remember, especially in connection with the line taken in the discussion of Catullus, that Lucretius' poetically revolutionary contemporary began his book by

---

criterion of reality. ... The criterion is a criterion of the exisistence or of the reality of particular things ... but it is also a criterion of truth and falsehood. This can only mean that the criterion may be used not only to judge problems about the possible existence or non-existence of objects in the world, but also to settle questions about the truth-value of propositions about such existent or non-existent objects."

calling it a "novum libellum" (1.1) and dedicated it to a man to whose *audacia* as a writer Catullus referred explicitly. Thus, for Lucretius the Hesiodic and Alexandrian associations of such phrasing would also have lain close to the surface, since his direct reference is to novelty of diction and subject in a poem and his words are followed so soon by the poetically loaded "laborem", as Catullus followed "novum libellum" and "ausus es" in his poem with "laboriosis" (1.7). The civic point becomes unambiguous in "virtus" and "suavis amicitiae". Suggestion of civic reform will flow not only from the picture given previously of "virtus" but from its association here with the talk of novelty and "sperata voluptas" immediately after. The implications are strengthened by the contrast between Greek and Latin cultures, repeated from "Graius homo" at 66, and the location of knowledge in Greek thought, particularly if we keep the contrary position of Cicero in mind.

The hope of this novel poem is a novel value, the realization of new purpose in life. The new poetry and the new life will be achieved through the enlightenment of the private intellect ("tuae ... menti") and a resulting true perception of reality, up to now hidden not only from view but from the Latin language and Roman ways ("res ... occultas"). The instrument of this enlightenment will not be the old education to *civitas*, based on the interpretation of life in the *mos maiorum*, but the location of *fides* in "naturae species" whose standard of interpretation will be *ratio*. Everything coheres. The philosophy is foundation and provocation of the poetry, whose end is intellectual and therefore civic revolution. The problem Lucretius has to solve is not philosophical—that has been solved already and is a given—but a matter of linguistic reform and literary revolution directed toward civic crisis.

Even if the description of these verses to this point be taken to sharpen and clarify the origin and thrust of 136-148, it must create a difficulty for understanding "novis verbis" at 138, since the interpretation offered claims that Lucretius' procedure is the redeployment of old words, not the creation of new ones. The style of the *De Rerum Natura* is inventive and even idiosyncratic.[23] It is characterized by new coinages, *hapax legomena* which are probably quite often Lucretian in origin, and borrowings from Greek vocabulary. What is to the present point, however, is that much of the invention and idiosyncrasy does not involve the creation of a new vocabulary, and so is irrelevant to understanding the passage,

---

[23] See Bailey (above, note 22) 132-171, for a survey of Lucretian style, on which I have relied for the information in this discussion, and W. S. Maguiness, "The Language of Lucretius" in D. R. Dudley (ed.), *Lucretius* (New York 1965) 69-93, which covers the same basic material and coheres with the point of view expressed here about Lucretius' inventiveness.

and that so little of what is new in the words involves the language of philosophical analysis. Coinages such as "frugiferentis", "largifluum", or "lauricomos" are literary in character, pretty much standard fare in the old Latin poetic style, and have no philosophical reference. Others, such as "adumbratim", "moderatim", "praecipitanter", "mactatus", "opinatus", and "summatus" are not only not particularly philosophical, they are formed on such normal rules of Latin morphology as to be transparent even when, and if, new. They are also hardly central to Lucretius' intellectual structure.

These and other features, including the elaborate periphrases, which often do have technical analytic reference, contribute to the abundance, difficulty, and richly personal character of Lucretius' style, but they do not fulfill the implied promise of a new philosophical vocabulary, the necessity for creating which increases the hardship of illuminating the dark discoveries of the Greeks. What is most striking about Lucretius' diction in this repect is its employment of familiar Latin words to express technical Epicurean concepts: e.g., *inane, res, natura, semina, corpora, primordia/principia, ratio, simulacra, imago, material/materies, spatium, species, concilium, plagae, motus, discidium, sensus, voluptas.* He does, of course, invent new terms such as *clinamen* and *momen* (though this may hardly be considered very new), but this is an unusual feature of his writing and by no means lives up to "multa novis verbis". And we do not get the justification of this promise if we add all the Greek words in the poem. They are not used to create a technical Epicurean vocabulary for Latin. By and large, they are literary and common or restricted to the narrow areas of meteorology or music and thus serve a very limited purpose, hardly touching the central issues or vast expanse of the *De Rerum Natura.*[24]

Using the old Latin words in fact increased the difficulty of communication for Lucretius, a difficulty which would have been lessened had he simply imported the established Greek terms for his principal technical categories. Had his purpose been purely explanatory, didactic, and descriptive, purely philosophical, this is what he should have done. Greek was well-known to his oligarchic audience—and the *De Rerum Natura* is nothing if not an oligarchic poem[25]—and it would have been no

---

[24] Compare M. P. O. Morford (above, note 17) for a discussion of Cicero's handling of some of the same problems in his *Aratea.*

[25] Here I agree with Kenney, *Lucretius* (above, note 18) 3, 7n.3, and see 4: "Now the one thing that cannot be said of the *D.R.N.* is that it is on the whole easy reading." Indeed not. Thus, against T. P. Wiseman, "The Two Worlds of Titus Lucretius", in *Cinna the Poet and Other Roman Essays* (Leicester 1974) 11-43. See B. Farrington, *The Faith of Epicurus* (above, note 8) 139, on the apparent contrast between the Epicurean prose propagandists and Lucretius. The *De Rerum Natura* shows the oligarchic education and culture. It is ad-

longer a task to indicate their technical meaning than that required by his
Latin words. He would have had the advantage of beginning with terms
that had no distracting references or distorting emotional associations,
and his explanations in Latin would have been controlled by the Greek
technical meanings. Ultimately, his presentation would have gained in
analytic clarity.[26]

Lucretius' decision not to adopt a Greek technical vocabulary posed a
problem for him, but it also sharpens our perception of his purpose,
which becomes comparable to the purposes of Catullus and Cicero. The
former solution would not have been literary, specifically poetic, and he
does want to write a poem. Beyond this, he wants his poem to revaluate
the literary heritage and rearrange Roman culture, to reform the
language itself and the society based on it. He does not simply want to set
out a philosophical system. He wants to create a direct effect for that
system on the pattern of life and thought. This cannot be accomplished
by ignoring the language that reflects and embeds the inherited social
form of thought and motivates a pattern of life it fossilizes and inspires. It
can only be accomplished by dealing with the traditional vocabulary (and
restructuring the relations of the words to one another) and with the
traditional literary forms (revaluating the worth and point of the various
kinds and their typical content). He can then also recapitulate the typical
Epicurean tactic of moving from the familiar to the unfamiliar[27]—in the
case of words, from the familiar erroneous meanings to new content
(which will refer to what is presently unfamiliar but true).

These considerations bring us to the reason Lucretius spends so much
time with *religio*. This name is the central category of the *mos maiorum*. If

---

dressed to an oligarch. The problems it raises are the problems of oligarchy (the evils of
nobilitas, not of the obscure life to which Epicureanism is the exhortation), and the solutions it offers are those available to oligarchs. Wiseman restates his position in "*Pete nobiles
amicos*: Poets and Patrons in Late Republican Rome", in B. K. Gold (ed.), *Literary and Artistic Patronage in Ancient Rome* (Austin 1982) 35-38. *Religio* is not the problem of the man in
the street, as Lucretius defines it. It is the underpinning of *nobilitas*, even if the *nobiles* do
not recognize this. His aim is to show the link, and by rendering *religio* vain and
ridiculous, by implicitly comparing the *nobiles* to the untutored *vulgus*, to show them that
therefore their whole pattern of life is intellectually no better than that of the lowest, most
uncultured element of society.

[26] Lucretius' approach to the problem of expressing new concepts by old words is
similar to Catullus' and seems to me to mitigate the force of Rubino's argument (above,
note 13), particularly on 293. Catullus may have had no choice about using the inherited
language, while Lucretius did, but Lucretius' choice and practice shows how far the
reinterpretation of old words was possible. I would argue that Catullus and Lucretius, in
their different aims, so far succeeded that it took Virgil a lifetime to put the inheritance
back into its old frame of reference (see below, section 8), with help from Horace and
Livy, hindered by the subversions of Propertius and Ovid.

[27] Compare Bailey (above, note 22) 58-59.

the poet can portray it as a snare and a delusion, the name of an empty set, if he can drain it of meaning, if he can separate it from *pietas*, which will then *require* a new definition in order to continue in use, then the house of ancient city thought, deprived of its jointures, will tumble. He will then have wakened his audience to his purpose, brought them to a consciousness of the sources of their ideas and actions, and reshaped the world before their eyes. Whether or not the oligarchs believed they still believed in the force of *religio*, their world view and pattern of life was rooted in it—perhaps even more firmly than if they had been aware of the fact. If the link between their world of ideas and *religio* can be shown, and if *religio* can be demolished as a category of analysis, then they will have no choice but to admit their ideas have no anchor in reality. There will be no choice but to find a new source of thought in a new account of reality, with the consequences of this new world view for their pattern of life.

If *religio* goes, a new theory about the way of the world is required. If that theory stems from an observation of nature and not the experience of *civitas*, then the centrality of *civitas* will go too, and with it the last claim to primacy of the *mos maiorum*. Employing Latin words enables Lucretius to make the link between idea and action, and to show the social consequences of his ideas. If he had used Greek technical terms or technical coinages, he could not have shown the way in which Roman values were tied to the language of social life and stemmed from the centrality of *religio*. As an intellectual strategy, the cleverness of this approach is enhanced if the oligarchs do not in fact take *religio* seriously anymore. If he shows that a term of analysis they admit to be vain is the foundation of their life, then their position is much more indefensible on their own terms than if he had attacked a still living idea. If, in addition, he can save many of the old categories by showing they have a true relation to reality and what that relation is, when reality is properly understood, he has much more chance of persuasion than if he attempts to void every word.

The same is true of Lucretius' approach to literature. He does not say that the story of Iphigeneia is false but that its point is not understood. Interpreted correctly, it is important evidence for the proper way of behavior and the evil of the old system. The interpretation is not allegorical but strictly historical. It does not find hidden meaning about the way of the world in the story but shows that the story requires a new, explicit account of that way. Literature does not have to be discarded or allegorized in order to save it as an activity. Its elements can be rearranged and reinterpreted to construct a new tradition which will give form to the Epicurean view of the world, similarly to the manner in which it had traditionally given form to civic knowledge and value. The wise man can not only discuss and interpret literature best, the wise man can write poetry.

From the First Proem on, Lucretius builds not simply a new world for the oligarchs, or a new literature for this world, but, necessarily, a new language for the description of reality and as the substance of its literature. He eliminates some categories as irredeemably empty of content or value: *religio*, *imperium*, and *civitas*. The last simply does not, for understandable reasons, exist in Lucretius and is dispensed with by being allowed no application in the real world. The only related word to occur is "civis", used to refer to the ordinary "citizens" who aid in the falsehearted and impious killing of Iphigeneia. So much for citizenry as a guarantee of truth, *fides*, *honor*, and *pietas*. *Imperium* finds its fate in Book 3 at verse 998, in the course of the diatribe that serves as the book's close. Sisyphus' ever vain toiling uphill with his rock is symbolic of the life of civic ambition. He stands for the man "qui petere a populo fascis saevasque securis / imbibit et semper victus tristisque recedit" (996-997), a not very complimentary portrait of the pattern of *civitas*, for the goal of the contest for civil honor is in truth an empty name: "nam petere imperium quod inanest nec datur umquam" (998). *Imperium* is a name without a reference in the world of things. It is, in Epicurean terms, part of the void.

Religio, although dismissed early on from the new language, is yet favored not only with mention elsewhere, mainly in the civic proems to the other five books but also with a lengthy treatment in the course of the satire on civic history in Book 5 at verses 1161-1240. *Religio* is a name not used there, but it is the subject of the description and denunciation, as Lucretius explains its historical origin. This is an event for which, he says, it is not difficult to present the rule of interpretation in words: "rationem reddere verbis" (1168). Lucretius' true interpretation (*ratio*) of the process by which *religio* grew is that it was based on the false understanding (i.e. *ratio*) by human beings of their true perceptions. Because people lacked the true principle of interpretation ("rationis egestas" at 1211) of evidence, they developed a false theory of reality, of which *religio* is the center.

Lucretius follows his purely historical interpretation with a satire or diatribe against this origin and the role of *religio* in human affairs (1194-1240), similar to his satirical intervention or Epicurean diatribe at 1117-1135, where he begins by asserting that *vera ratio* will lead to correct conclusions about what is true wealth, and 1148-1160. While much of the comment is universal in application, the Roman and civic point is prominent: "induperatorem classis" (1227), "legionibus" (1228—although "elephantis" here incorporates foreigners into the picture), "divum pacem votis'' (1229), ''pulchros fascis saevasque securis'' (1234). The reader is reminded, by implication and allusion, that *religio* is the heart and foundation of civic life. All is shown vain and frustrate. The civil allusions draw out the point at the beginning of the satirical comment at 1194-1203, for Lucretius started from the ridicule of the specific forms of *religio Romana*: ''velatum'' (1198), ''ad lapidem'' (1199), ''accedere ad aras'' (1199), ''procumbere humi prostratum et pandere palmas'' (1200), ''aras sanguine multo / spargere quadrupedem nec votis nectere vota'' (1201-1202). While some of this language could have wider application in the life of the ancient city, ''velatum'' is clearly Roman and no Roman reader could fail to imagine anything other than the familiar rites of Roman citizenry.[28] In any case, Lucretius' explicit point dictates the reference to Rome: the definition of the category *pietas*. He starts with ''nec pietas ullast'' (1198) and then shows what *pietas* is not. As in the Iphigeneia passage, it is not observation and performance of the rules of *religio*. Here, however, he goes on to give a positive definition of the category: ''sed mage pacata posse omnia mente tueri'' (1203)—''But more is it the ability to watch everthing with an ordered (i.e. serene) intellect.'' This is the Epicurean salvation of *pietas*, giving Lucretius' destructive description a positive product. He then proceeds to illustrate the futility of prayer (1229) and the vanity of civic forms before the real working of the world—which must reshape the understanding of his prayer for civic peace at the opening of the poem.

The separation of *pietas* from the civic structure, begun in the First Proem and completed with a positive uncivil definition in Book 5, also played a role in the proem to Book 3, where it is associated as a candidate for redemption with *amicitia*.[29] At verses 3.31-90, Lucretius discourses once more on the common pattern of civic life, the evil it represents, and the source of that pattern and its evils in a false account of the world: the notion of Acheron and *religio* with the attendant fear of death. This is perhaps the clearest statement in the poem that the form of civic life stems from *religio* and the explanation it offers of the working of the world. The fear of death, which is a part, or result, or cause of *religio* leads to the

---

[28] So Bailey (above, note 22) on 5.1198-1203, and 1198 in particular, against which P. Boyancé, ''Velatum...ad lapidem'', *Latomus* 35 (1976) 550-554, arguing for reference to a Greek custom, is not convincing in context here or the general ambience of the poem.

[29] On piety and the other Epicurean ''virtues'', see N. W. DeWitt (above, note 10) 249-288 and 289-327, but also B. Farrington, *The Faith of Epicurus* (above, note 8) 20-32 (''Friendship versus Justice'') and Rist, *Epicurus: An Introduction* (above, note 22) 127-139 (''The Problem of Friendship''). A contemporary discussion of the Epicurean virtues is found in Torquatus' exposition in Cicero's *De Finibus* 1.42-70, and particularly 65-70, an account of debate among Epicureans themselves over *amicitia*.

destruction of all moral value: "hunc vexare pudorem, hunc vincula amicitiai / rumpere et in summa pietatem evertere suadet" (83-84). *Amicitia* and *pudor*, along with *pietas*, are separated from civic order. *Religio*, instead of being their support and justification, destroys them.

The rest of the proem to Book 3 undertakes the same task of intellectual revolution. The terms in which Epicurus is praised at the very beginning of the book are famous, but the civil implications give that praise its contemporary point and ethical force: "tu *pater* es, rerum inventor, tu *patria* nobis / suppeditas praecepta" (8-9), and it is Epicurus' "aurea dicta" (12) which are "dignissima" (13). Not the *mos maiorum*, not the *pater familias*, not the civic *patres*, not the *dignitas* of Republican *honor*, not even the civic poet *pater* Ennius, but Epicurus is the source of wisdom, knowledge, and worth. This is a new version of paternal authority, and a new source of *dignitas*, leading to "quaedam divina voluptas" at verse 28. The description of Epicurus' achievement and its implications for civic reform are linked with the goal of reforming the inherited literature in verses 19-22: the reapplication of the quotation from *Odyssey* 6.42-46 on the abodes of the gods to a new and Epicurean purpose. From this, Lucretius proceeds to his standard dismantling of the *mos maiorum*, and we may note, in addition to the points already made his references to the *parentalia* ("parentant" at 51), "manibu' divis" (52), "inferias" (53), "religionem" (54), "honorum caeca cupido" (59), "sanguine civili" (70), "caedem caede accumulantes" (71), "potentem" (75), "claro ... honore" (76), "statuarum et nominis ergo" (78), and "patriam carosque parentis" (85). Those who perish "for the sake of a name" are perishing for nothing but the names of empty sets in the civic order of thought, as "nominis ergo" must allude to the Lucretian theme of the relationship between *nomina* and *res*—compare the account of the origin of "rerum...nomina" (5.1051) in Book 5, a theme of the age as a whole.

Religio, *imperium*, *civitas*, *pietas*, *amicitia*, and *pudor* take on new roles in the world, divorced from their old coherent structure. New words are elevated to the status of fundamental categories. The source of *fides* is shifted from *civitas* to *natura*, from social to private knowledge, from, as it were, history to "logic" (in its most general sense of rationalistic argument), or, better, from authority to reason.[30] *Fides* is always anchored in sense perception in Lucretius: "quid maiore fide porro quam sensus habere / debet?" (4.482-483.) It is linked with *ratio* and the new *salus* at 4.500-506:

---

[30] *De Rerum Natura* 5.1133-1135: "quandoquidem sapiunt alieno ex ore petuntque / res ex auditis potius quam sensibus ipsis, / nec magis id nunc est neque erit mox quam fuit ante."

et si non poterit ratio dissolvere causam,
cur ea quae fuerint iuxtim quadrata, procul sint
visa rutunda, tamen praestat rationis egentem
reddere mendose causas utriusque figurae,
quam manibus manifesta suis emittere quoquam
et violare fidem primam et convellere tota
fundamenta quibus nixatur vita salusque.

Here *ratio* must be "rule of interpretation", or the canonic, and *salus* is not the welfare of the *cives* of the *civitas* but an individual wellbeing grounded in the facts of nature properly interpreted. So, the redefinition of *salus* perhaps hinted at in the First Proem has by this point been given positive substance by its own anchoring in the new reality.

Ius is demoted from the status of a category of analysis to an ordinary word. It appears eight times in the *De Rerum Natura*, and its adjective twice. Five of these appearances are as the idiom (or dead metaphor) *iure* and have no analytic significance. The form *iura* appears twice, three verses apart in Book 5 (1144 and 1147), in the account of the establishment of civil society and its laws, where it is used to refer to a stage of activity in history and not as a term of analysis. It is not differentiated from *leges*, in conjunction with which it occurs both times. *Iuris* occurs at 3.61 in the phrase "transcendere finis / iuris", which, in context, refers to illegal campaigning and means little more than "breaking the law".

This interpretation gains support from the occurrences of *iustus*. At 3.950, in the rebuke of man's fear of death by Nature, the phrase is "iustam intendere litem", a metaphor from the sphere of legal action and not analytical. The phrase "praeter iustum" at 4.1241 comes from the description of sterility and is nothing more than a casual idiom. Once again, then, the poet redefines a basic civic category, in this case not draining it of content or shifting its reference but rendering it intellectually trivial by depriving it of analytic function. This is precisely opposite to the Ciceronian position, in which *ius* plays a central role as the link between the natural and social orders, and perfectly consonant with standard Epicurean thought.[31]

The case of *virtus* is at first more ambiguous. Verses 1.70 and 1.140, referring first to Epicurus' achievement and secondly associating the word with *voluptas*, suggest a redefinition in Epicurean terms parallel to much that was happening to the word in other contemporary thought. This potential, however, is never developed. At 5.858 and 863, *virtus* refers simply to the physical aggressiveness of animals, a demotion or

---

[31] See Rist (above, note 22) 122-124 and Farrington, *The Faith of Epicurus* (above, note 8) 20-32.

trivialization even greater than that meted out to *ius*. How can an animal have "manhood"? This is an application of *virtus* to which Cicero objects openly: "Nam nec arboris nec equi virtus, quae dicitur, in quo abutimur nomine, in opinione sita est, sed in natura." (*De Legibus* 1.45.) Here again a sharp line divides Cicero and Lucretius, as Cicero rebukes the manner in which Lucretius and others demean the name of civil manhood. At 5.966, *virtus* is used of human beings in the primitive stage of development with a meaning scarcely more elevated than bestial forwardness. This leaves 2.642, where the reference is traditional ("virtute velint patriam defendere terram") but is part of the allegorical interpretation of the rites of the Magna Mater immediately to be rejected (645), as repudiated by the true rule of interpretation ("a vera ratione repulsa").

While, therefore, the First Proem leads us to expect something from *virtus* of the sort we get with *pietas, amicitia*, and *fides*, nothing comes of our expectations. Like *civitas* and *ius*, *virtus* proves uninteresting and unuseful to Lucretius the Epicurean. *Civitas* is the order he wishes to destroy, and *ius* and *virtus*, while not as noxious as *religio*, were too much pillars of that order to be securely separable from it. They could not be saved for Epicurean analysis, and, indeed, had no Epicurean utility, since *rerum natura* and *ratio*, and the denial of divine providence, left no place for *ius*, and redefinition of *virtus* as *voluptas*, or an effect of *voluptas*, would have been, at best, an otiose exercise. *Voluptas* is the required concept and leaves nothing important for *virtus* to do.[32]

This consideration of Lucretius' intellectual vocabulary has still not advanced solution of the problem of "multa novis verbis" at 1.138. It adds justification, as if justification were needed, for the claim of "rerum novitatem" and the complaint of "egestatem linguae" at 1.139, but we have not yet found new words. On the basis of what Lucretius actually does, we should have expected a phrase like "multa nova patriis verbis", but this is not what he says. It is, however, about what he must have had in mind. At least it represents the real difficulty with which he dealt and the actual accomplishment of his poem. Lucretius creates his new world mainly by the new use of old words, using the inherited names in novel ways and with new relations to one another—promoting, demoting, and transferring to new assignments—to explain his many new things. Novelty of rank and application, "words used in new ways", is not what

---

[32] Compare Rist (above, note 22) 125 and DeWitt (above, note 10) 245-248 ("The Relation of Pleasure to Virtue"). For *vera voluptas* as goal and standard, note *De Rerum Natura* 5.1433. Also compare Cicero's litany of the old words in the section from the introduction to the *De Re Publica* quoted in the text above, section 6.

"novis verbis" means, but it is what the phrase refers to, if it has any reference at all.

The larger result of this account of Lucretius' assault on the civic categories is an explanation of the structure of the poem, and ultimately of the relation of that structure to its literary form and Lucretius' literary ambition. In this light, the observations on the nature of Latin and the poet's linguistic difficulties become central to his work in its historical context and as a document in intellectual history. His concern with *religio* becomes fundamental not only to Lucretius' imagination and personality but to his impersonal task. We begin to see that Lucretius must demonstrate that even those people who think they disregard portions of the inheritance of knowledge (e.g., *religio*) only ignore certain inconveniences of that heritage. Their fundamental way of looking at the world, as shown by their pattern of life and value, is the old way. They, more perhaps than others, must be shown the interdependence of the parts, that, if one goes, all must go, and so they must be taught the analytical and ethical consequences of their own indifference, an indifference whose significance they clearly do not themselves understand. The perception of the poet's awareness of the civic roots of the system of knowledge he must destroy, if he is to win a way for Epicureanism, and therefore of the necessarily civic purpose of the poem, sharpens perception of the way in which Lucretius has arranged his material and gives intellectual significance to the pattern.

Each of the six books of the *De Rerum Natura* begins with a civic proem to set the context and goal and predict the effect of the Epicurean description to follow. This includes the proem to Book 4, when the relation between Lucretius' literary ambition and his civil point is understood, though, admittedly, some special argument is required to place this proem in a civic context. Each of the last four books also closes with a satire on civic life,[33] setting them off from the first two books. We have now lain the foundation for asking the point of this pattern and for illuminating the civic purpose in those sections where it might not be clear immediately, for example, the ends of Books 4 and 6. We have looked already at the proems to Books 1 and 3. A glance at the others will draw out into stronger relief the nature and extent of the poem's statement of

---

[33] On Lucretius and satire, see: H. P. Houghton, "Lucretius as Satirist", *TAPA* 43 (1912) xxxiv-xxxix; C. Murley, "Lucretius and Roman Satire", *TAPA* 67 (1936) xliv; C. Murley, "Lucretius and the History of Satire", *TAPA* 70 (1939) 380-395; R. Waltz, "Lucrèce satirique", *Lettres d'humanité* 8 (1949) 78-103; D. R. Dudley, "The Satiric Element in Lucretius" in D. R. Dudley (above, note 23), 115-130; B. P. Wallach, *Lucretius and the Diatribe Against the Fear of Death* (Leiden 1976); and E. J. Kenney, *Lucretius: De Rerum Natura Book III* (above, note 19), especially 17-20 and 199-244. The last two are fundamental explorations of the topic.

its frame of reference and aims and bring the outlines of the satires into focus.

In the proem to Book 2, Lucretius advocates the philosophical withdrawal and spirit of detachment criticized by Cicero. Nothing is sweeter than the abstention from the contest for *nobilitas*, which Cicero condemns as the lack of *virtus*. Instead of the mark of greatness and worth in life, the struggle for *honor* is the product of wretchedness of intellect and blindness of heart. *Nobilitas* is thereby removed as a value. The poet then tells us that the desire for wealth is vanity, and we are exhorted to life according to uncivilized—i.e. not primitive or bestial, but uncitied or unpoliticized—nature. This is the radical denunciation of the value of civil culture and a claim for the radical unreality, emptiness, of civic categories, summed up in verses 37-39:

> quapropter quoniam nil nostro in corpore gazae
> proficiunt neque nobilitas nec gloria regni,
> quod superest, animo quoque nil prodesse putandum.

Social institutions are founded on ethical delusion. They are not natural, in the sense that they do not flow from nature's demands and so are not connected to nature by knowledge. They are the product of human impositions upon nature. They are not real, in the sense that they originate in delusory dreams about the real nature of the world, from a false rule of interpretation of the significance of our real perceptions. They are "natural" in the modern, English sense of that word, in its equivocal references, but this is an English problem with categories of analysis, not Lucretius'. A distinction must be made between what is natural, in the sense of deriving from knowledge of the order of nature, and what is usual in human behavior, which may derive from ignorance of reality. Something may be often, even always, the case, without being natural in the normative Epicurean sense, or joined to reality by knowledge. Only the world of uncivilized nature (in the meaning of the Classical concept and not the English category "primitive") is real. The rest of the proem extends the criticism of the emptiness of the civic forms in its talk of "legiones per loca campi" (40), "belli" (41), "classem" (43a), "religiones" (44), "sonitus armorum ... fera tela" (49), "inter reges rerumque potentis" (50), "purpureai" (52). The cure for the distress of life is, of course, observation of nature and the rule of interpretation: "naturae species ratioque" (61).

While we can allow the Second Proem to remind us of the Ciceronian ideal, the target is more properly the unrefined civic life, not the sophisticated Ciceronian defense. We should think more of the spectacular careers of the famous cosmopolitan politicians (careers oxymoronic in name as they were paradoxical in fact) of the Late Republic: Great Pompey, Lucullus, Crassus, Verres, Gabinius, L. Calpurnius Piso Caesoninus, C. Memmius, and, of course, C. Julius Caesar.

The Fifth Proem continues and refines the Lucretian contrast between the two fundamental sources of knowledge set up by the poem, the civic and the Epicurean. On the one hand, the mythology of the old religion tells us that great gifts of knowledge and order were bestowed by Ceres, Liber, and Hercules. The last Lucretius demeans particularly. Many of his labors are listed and ridiculed, not because the stories about them are false but because the labors were insignificant. As in the Iphianassa passage, the facts have not been estimated correctly: "Herculis antistare si facta putabis / longius a vera multo ratione ferere" (21-22). If you will judge that the deeds of Hercules are more important than those of Epicurus, you will be carried much further away from the true interpretation than you were in evaluating the gifts of Ceres and Liber. In his role as the symbol of the process of civilization, of the establishment of order, and as the great servant of mankind, Hercules is the quintessentially civil hero, which will lead Virgil, in one of his many rebukes of Lucretius, to make so much of him in *Aeneid* 8. If Lucretius is attacking Stoicism and its accomodation to the ethic of the *mos maiorum* anywhere, it must be here, and no noble reader could fail to think of Stoicism at this point. But if this is attack, it is only by implication and extension, since the poet's real target is *civitas*. If that can be destroyed, the Stoic accomodations are nullified automatically.[34]

---

[34] The question of Lucretius and Stoicism is allied to the larger question of his philosophical originality. On this subject, see especially: P. H. DeLacy, "Lucretius and the History of Epicureanism", *TAPA* 79 (1948) 12-23; D. J. Furley, "Lucretius and the Stoics", *BICS* 13 (1966) 13-33; K. Kleve, "The Philosophical Polemics in Lucretius", *Entretiens Hardt* XXIV (Genève 1978) 39-75; D. J. Furley, "Lucretius the Epicurean" (above, note 21) in the same volume; and P. H. DeLacy, "Lucretius and Plato" in Συζήτησις: *Studi sull'Epicureismo greco e romano offerti a Marcello Gigante* 291-307. A. D. Winspear (above, note 10), 1-15, makes an argument for Lucretian originality which seems to me to amount to little more than praise of his inventive style and presentation. The fragmentary state of the sources does not easily allow any argument to be made for the philosophical originality of Lucretius. We must either claim nothing for Lucretius himself, on the basis of a necessary historical agnosticism, or, if we make a claim from the evidence, we must say Lucretius made no original contribution to philosophy, whether or not he got everything from Epicurus. Everything in DeLacy's "Lucretius and Plato", for instance, seems to me able to have come from Epicurus himself. Compare the relationship of Plato to Epicurus portrayed by Farrington in *The Faith of Epicurus* (above, note 8) and *Science and Politics* (above, note 8) 130-147. See Furley's conclusion to his "Lucretius and the Stoics" (31-32), especially his final sentence, on Lucretius (32): "Wisely, or perhaps just luckily, he avoided these side issues and concentrated his fire on the main enemy: *De Rerum Natura* is the Atomists' answer to the Aristotelian world-picture." This will cohere with the description of the world view of the First Century B.C. found in Thornton (above, note 7). Both Thornton and Furley will serve to place Lucretius in his proper in-

If, on the other hand, we identify the source of knowledge with
divinity, then Epicurus was a god. In the course of Lucretius' extrapolation of the praise of Epicurus from the Third Proem, he strengthens the
assertion that he is the source of what is called wisdom ("sapientia" at
verse 10) because he is the man who *first* discovered the principle of
understanding life, "vitae rationem" (9).[35] All knowledge comes from
Epicurus, and no tales of the gods embedded in the civic account as the
justification of its forms and *religiones* can compete with this. This is the
point Lucretius develops in verses 56-90, where he contrasts the
Epicurean account of the evidence about reality with that of civil *religio*:
"neve aliqua divum volvi ratione putemus" (81) and "rursus in antiquas
referuntur religiones" (86). Lucretius also revives the linguistic theme,
particularly of the origin of names of things: "quove modo genus
humanum variante loquella / coeperit inter se vesci per nomina rerum"
(71). In all of this, the poet also stresses his own literary ambition and
concomitant lack of philosophical pretension. He is writing a poem:
"Quis potis est dignum pollenti pectore carmen / condere pro rerum

---

tellectual context and explain the reason for the persistence of his attack on *religio* and the
notion of divine providence, both of which were the categorical pillars of the fundamental
ideas about the universe among the intellectual class, and among the mass, of the Late
Republic. Plato and Aristotle erected the defense of an intellectually refined civic heritage.
This is why Epicurus attacked their conclusions, however much he also borrowed. This
attack Lucretius transferred to Rome. He did not attack the Stoics or other late anti-
Epicurean arguments directly, because he was not a creative philosophical thinker (he was
a creative poetic thinker) and because he did not have to. His enemy was *civitas Romana* as
an intellectual structure. If he could destroy that, what need was there to bother with subsidiary defenses of what had been demolished? They would go the way of the nullified
system. Lucretius was in the forefront of the intellectual controversy of his time, but as a
poet not as analytical thinker. Philosophically, while Lucretius of course knew and knew
of the schoolmen, in the narrow world of oligarchy and its Greek dependents, he was
isolated from their school structure and took no part in their debates. He and Catullus
lived in the same literary world, for that was where their talents lay.
    Reference should perhaps also be made to J. H. Nichols, Jr., *Epicurean Political
Philosophy* (Ithaca 1976), which covers much of the conceptual material of this essay.
Nichols' discussion seems to me, however, to be too little rooted in the realities of
historical developments in the Classical world, Roman society, and Greek and Latin
words to be of much use in understanding more than the surface shape of Lucretius' pattern of thought. He does not take us very far into the literary, historical, and intellectual
depths of the poem This leads to an unsatisfactory account throughout of Lucretius' attitude to "politics", and his demonstration of Lucretian atheism (148-167) appears not
only to misconceive the method of the poem (and wrongly to interpret Lucretius on
analytic grounds), but to misunderstand the nature of the debate over the gods (which
turned more on the issue of divine providence than divine existence) and the nature of ancient (civic) religion and its connection with "politics". Indeed, in any discussion of
"religion" in Lucretius, *pietas* must be considered as much as *religio* and direct mention of
the gods, and *pietas* is saved by Lucretius in an Epicurean sense. This will save part of
"religion". Indeed, in the *De Rerum Natura*, the enemy is *religio*, not "religion".
    [35] See D. J. Furley, "Lucretius the Epicurean" (above, note 21) 6-9.

maiestate hisque repertis?'' (1-2.) The goal is to write one worthy of the philosophical insight he has wholly derived from another: ''Cuius ego ingressus vestigia dum rationes / persequor ac doceo dictis'' (54-55). Epicurus is the new source of knowing and understanding from which everyone, including Lucretius, will now derive his conception of reality and value.

If Epicurus and his system are to replace civic divinity and its mythology as the foundation of life, it would contradict Lucretius' purpose, as shown by all he has said about Epicurus as *deus* and the exaltation of his accomplishment above the reputations of Ceres, Liber, and Hercules, for the poet to claim philosophic ambition. Lucretius is to be the new Homer, or Ennius, the founder of the new literature of Epicureanism, i.e. an entirely new literary tradition that will be for Epicureanism what Homer and Ennius were for *civitas*. It is here that we see not only the coalescence of the civic and literary goals of the poem, that they are sides of the same Lucretian coin, since it is impossible in the Classical world for literature, as part of the unified and indivisible civic inheritance, not to have civic ramifications, but also therefore the civic significance of Book 1.921-950, verses 926-950 of which are repeated as the proem to Book 4. While philosophically Lucretius traces the tracks of Epicurus (''ingressus vestigia'' at 5.55), poetically he sets out over trackless places, where no one has walked before: ''avia Pieridum peragro loca nullius ante / trita solo'' (926-927). His attempt and inspiration are novel: ''integros...fontes'' (927), ''novos...flores'' (928), and ''unde prius nulli velarint tempora musae'' (930). The novelty is double: of subject and purpose. He is writing poetry on an obscure subject: ''obscura de re tam lucida pango / carmina'' (933-934). His purpose is not the expression of the values of civic life but the overthrow of its foundations: ''religionum animum nodis exsolvere'' (932).

It is not the aim of this essay to argue the question of the relationship between Epicureanism and poetry. The clear facts do, however, invite conclusions. Lucretius added a literary dimension to Epicureanism, and in this he was novel both as an Epicurean and as a poet. To this point, there had been no poetic rendition of Epicurean doctrines. Lucretius' motivation, aside from his ambition to do something new as a poet, stemmed entirely from the pressure of the poem's civic purpose. He clearly believed that if Epicureanism was to take root in society at large, specifically in Roman society, it must reach out to the wider audience in the form and on the terms to which that audience was used. Just as Epicureanism could not have had full effect until the *civitas* was enlightened about the real foundation of its view of the world in *religio*, so also it could not take root while, no matter what people said they believed, their culture, including their literary culture, was civil. Just as it was necessary to replace the old source of knowing and the old standard of interpretation, so it was necessary to replace the old poetry.

It may have been the civic character of the inherited literature, as much as the inadequacy of poetic expression for analytic argument, that caused Epicurus to say that the wise man will not write poetry, believing that poetry could have only one ethic.[36] Since it was also analytically useless, there could be no point in it. If so, Lucretius is saying that all of life must have an Epicurean character, if life is to be lived according to Epicurean principles. He attempts to save this position philosophically by the famous simile of the physicians' honied cups of medicine, a simile he would never have constructed if there had not been a need to justify the writing of an Epicurean philosophical poem. His claim to novelty in this regard is correct, and it is a novelty he expected would create some surprise and discomfort. Whether or not the writing of philosophical poetry does in fact contradict basic Epicurean attitudes, it does contradict the history of Epicurean practice, and for that practice there must have been a reason fundamental to the history of philosophy since Socrates as well as to Epicureanism in particular. Lucretius' position will, then, have had potential theoretical ramifications, if the schoolmen paid any attention to his work as an authentic Epicurean document, which is hardly likely, but they are ramifications he does not work out—and could not have, if he were to live up to his claim to trace the tracks of Epicurus.[37]

Analysis and art are two fundamentally different and differing modes of knowing. Epicurus recognized the former and not the latter. Lucretius seems to have believed that poetry can tell the truth and communicate authentic knowledge. The difficulties here are enormous and intricate, and they do not seem likely to be moved toward solution by any of several lines of periphrastic special pleading that end, wherever they begin, by blurring an utterly basic and crucially important distinction, that was also of great historical importance in Classical thought for the exponents of the claims of philosophy, rhetoric, and poetry, at least since the time of

---

[36] Diogenes Laertius 10.120; Plutarch, Mor. 1086f-1087a; Cicero, De Finibus 1.72, Torquatus' praise of Epicurus: "An ille tempus aut in poetis evolvendis, ut ego et Triarius te hortatore facimus, consumeret, in quibus nulla solida utilitas omnisque puerilis est delectatio... ." See DeWitt (above, note 10) 107-108, but the example of Philodemus is neither here nor there with regard to Lucretius.

[37] That is, he could not claim to be both a faithful follower of Epicurus and argue a role for poetry contrary to Epicurus' ideas. It is doubtful, of course, if Lucretius could have invented an analytically satisfactory argument by himself. There is a difference between feeling something to be true, even knowing it to be true, and being able to demonstrate its truth analytically with arguments of one's own invention cast in an acceptable logical form. Putting arguments in clear logical form does not seem to have been among Lucretius' talents. It certainly was not his aim.

Plato and Isokrates up to Philodemus, not to draw the line beyond the age of Lucretius.[38] One result of recognizing this distinction and controversy is that it sharpens our perception of the civic origin of the poetic claims in the *De Rerum Natura*, and the interdependence of the Epicurean subject, the theme of poetry, and the civic purpose. In this light, the civil character of the Fourth Proem becomes clear and gains in force.

The civic theme of the proems reaches its climax in the Sixth, where Lucretius evaluates the greatest of the old-style cities. Like Ceres, Liber, Hercules, and others, Athens had a famous reputation and made great claims for its benefits to humanity. It was far and away the grandest representative and example of the accomplishment and value of civic life. Lucretius admits these gifts of knowledge and adds one more: Epicurus. Whatever the other and earlier presents of Athens, mankind was left still in care and lamentation: "anxia corda" (14) and "saevire querellis" (16). It was Epicurus who showed the truth about life and its proper goal, marking out the path by which mankind ought to walk. This makes him, not its civic pattern, Athens' greatest gift, the man who, ironically, came to show the limits and failings in Athens' past accomplishments.

The rest of the proem sets out again the relationship of Epicureanism, civic aim, and poetic ambition (43-95). Again and again, Lucretius stresses the importance of a proper *ratio* of phenomena: "ratioque" (41), "nulla ratione" (56), "qua ratione" (59), "ratione" (66), "caeca ratione" (67), "verissima ratio" (80), "ratio [terrae] caelique tenenda" (83), "nulla ratione" (90). It is *caeca ratio* that leads men in their ignorance back into "antiquas...religiones" (62), from which the poem is designed to free them by application of *verissima ratio*. From this process there will arise a new definition for another category, *pax deorum*: "pacis eorum" (69).[39] The notion of true peace is as central to the passage as *ratio*: "placato" (49), "pacis" (69), "placida cum pace" (73), "placido" (75), "tranquilla pace" (78). The employment of true *ratio* and the redefinition of *pax* will be secured by the final destruction of *religio* in the new poetry: "sunt ornanda politis / versibus" (82-83). Lucretius closes with an invocation to Calliope, who is defined as "requies" and "voluptas" (94), the Epicurean and literary sum of the passage, and with the reiteration of his poetic ambition: "ut insigni capiam cum laude coronam" (75).

Book 6 is Athens' book, and it ends where it began. The closing section must be interpreted in terms of the book's beginning and in light of the method of the whole, which method is the same here as elsewhere. After

---

[38] See Minyard (above, note 18) 1-7 and 96-102.
[39] Compare "divum pacem" at 5.1229.

the proem on Athens and Epicurus, the poet presents the true way of interpreting those phenomena which impinge most directly upon daily life. These include, for the Egyptians, the flooding of the Nile, and pestilential lakes, and lead up to the general account of disease and the Great Plague at Athens (1138-1286). Why close with Athens and the Plague? This obviously makes the end cohere with the subject and pattern of the book, but the answer is once more found in civic purpose. The final section is a satire or diatribe against Athenian life.

Lucretius has just presented the true, Epicurean account of disease. But the Plague occurred in Athens before the birth of Epicurus. So, all the best of the old cities could rely on to deal with the overwhelming assault of the real (natural) world was the knowledge it then owned, its system of civic forms and responses. This did not give any true understanding or way of dealing with the crisis. All the citizens ("civibus" at 1140) could employ were those forms of thought that increased their panic and proved the intellectual and moral futility of their inheritance. Indeed, the passage is proof of what Lucretius says Epicurus found in the life of man when he looked about him, proof of the failure of the old way of truth.

The preceding account in the book establishes the standard of interpretation on which the satire is to be based: "haec ratio quondam morborum" (1138). Without this true account, the reader would not be able to perceive the satirical thrust of the description, its Epicurean point, or that the failure of polity is the subject. Just as Epicurus found men with "anxia corda" (14) and raging with lamentations ("saevire querellis" at 16), so the reaction to the plague was characterized by "anxius angor" (1158) and "gemitu commixta querella" (1159). Those weary with disease uttered appealing cries mingled with lament: "blandaque lassorum vox mixta voce querellae" (1245). Nothing they knew how to do, none of the great Athenian gifts, enabled them to deal with the plague, understand its causes, or adopt the proper attitude. Their science was helpless: "mussabat tacito medicina timore" (1179). Some of the sick mutilated their bodies from that fear of death, in the folly of which the poem has long instructed us: "et graviter partim metuentes limina leti" (1208) and "mortis metus...acer" (1212). The disaster even brought to some a loss of what had been known: "atque etiam quosdam cepere oblivia rerum / cunctarum" (1213-1214). The forms of civic life, convicted now of emptiness and pointlessness, were abandoned: "incomitata rapi certabant funera vasta" (1225), "nec iam religio divum nec numina magni / pendebantur" (1276-1277), and "nec mos ille sepulturae remanebit in urbe" (1278). The shrines and temples of the gods were piled high with the bodies of the dead their *religio* could not save. *Religio* ends the poem, as it began it, and in the way it began it. In the breakdown of *civitas*, all the structure of harmony and order was lost: "perturbatus enim totus" (1280) and "multo cum sanguine saepe / rixantes" (1285-1286).

This was the state of affairs at Athens, even Athens, before Epicurus told men the truth. Without the preceding description of the way of the world and the earlier civic criticism, we could not see the point of this closing picture. It is more than the tale of disaster. There is a reason for the way men behaved. They were left abandoned intellectually and morally by the way of life that was supposed to give them the method of understanding and dealing with the world. Here truly is the final bankruptcy of *religio*, when the temples have become the warehouses of the products of its failure. The point of this ending is contained in the Book's proem. *Civitas* is empty. It stands convicted of futility. Mankind waits for Epicurus and his truth.

The method of Book 6 flows from that in Books 3-5 and the foundation of the general *ratio naturae* set in Books 1 and 2. In all cases, the Epicurean narrative of nature is necessary for understanding the civic satire, and the civic satire lets the Epicurean natural narrative play a role in the contemporary intellectual crisis at Rome. In this way, the *De Rerum Natura* is far more than an *Epicurea*, has far more importance and deeper significance for its period than Sallustius' *Empedoclea* and Cicero's *Aratea*, which enrich Roman culture with Greek but do not challenge a way of life or offer a solution to the challenge of a crisis of institution and idea.

Satire, if it is to be effective, requires an understanding on the part of his audience of an author's standard of value and truth, the standard against which the object of satire is measured. It does not depend on an agreement between author and audience about the validity of the standard, but it does need clear perception of what the standard is, if his comments are to be seen as satire, as anything more than a kind of floating bitterness. Lucretius could and did draw on his readers' acquaintance with the long tradition of Hellenistic popular ethical criticism as a frame of reference,[40] as, for example, in the diatribes that close Books 3 and 4 and in the references to the standard vices at the beginning of Book 5: "superbia", "spurcitia", "petulantia", "luxus", "desidia" (47-48). This is the frame within which Epicurean moral criticism could also be located, but, if the poet were to make his own criticism of *civitas* and its *mos* specifically Epicurean, to insist that these evils were proof of the need for Epicureanism and that Epicureanism was their only cure, he had to do much more than that.

---

[40] See Wallach and Kenney (above, note 33).

What had to be done was to make his satire flow from an Epicurean account of reality. Lucretius does not simply criticize the world of the
citizen for being false to its own standards or false to standards of rational
behavior in general. He does not offer a catalogue of isolated follies or
even the description of a pattern of folly. He criticizes the intellectual
foundation of citizenry by presenting a rival interpretation of reality, the
effect of which he deepens and sharpens by rearranging the world of his
audience before its eyes, by reshaping the structure of their language for
describing reality. He rearranges the perceived relationship between
words and things. The consequence of his strategy is that the tradition of
satire on civic life is made to confirm Epicureanism, to be an added proof
of not only the necessity for some alternative but for this alternative. In
this respect, he uses the diatribe and the satirical themes in the way he
used Iphigeneia and the quotation from the *Odyssey* at 3.19-22: the inherited literature, properly understood, contains evidence for the non-
civic truth of Epicureanism. While the satirical description of city life, i.e.
the recognition of its ignorance and folly, is made a conclusion of argument drawn from Epicurean knowledge, and Epicurean knowledge itself
is made a conclusion of psychological need drawn from the observed in-
sufficiency of civic life. The satire becomes consequence and justification
of Epicurean doctrine.

Lucretius thus controls the response of his audience to his satire by
rooting that satire firmly in an Epicurean narrative. Books 1 and 2 set out
the fundamental structure of nature, to which all the description in Books
3-6 is subsidiary. This is the absolutely necessary foundation of
knowledge, before anything else about nature or politics can be said, but
by the end of Book 2 we are presented with conclusions closer to the
events and feelings of ordinary life. As we have seen, the proems to 1 and
2 have already established an ethical dimension for the poem, and Books
3-6 open with similar proems. Then, the description in Book 3 of the true
nature of the soul, including its mortality, lays the basis for the satire on
the fear of death and punishment in the Underworld and of related follies
of civic life. The satire on the passion and literature of love, with concluding advice on sex and procreation, in Book 4 is founded in the
description of sensation and human psychology which comprises the
book's Epicurean narrative. Lucretius' narration of the origin and
growth of the universe in Book 5 provides the framework for his description of the origin of human life and the history of human culture. In this
historical satire, he presents the stages by which the follies of contemporary life, described here and in the satires that close Books 3 and 4,
arose through deviations from the life according to nature. Book 6 pic-
tures the real status of those specific natural phenomena most obviously

part of human life, including disease, which allows Lucretius to narrow the historical focus of his satire from Book 5, as he has narrowed the natural focus of his descriptions, to the single, representative example of Athens.

The diatribe against the fear of death that closes Book 3 is not obviously civic or Roman in its point. This fear is made the cause, however, of the patterns of behavior found in citizenship, and these patterns keep surfacing as objects of criticism, as the outcome of this brand of ignorant folly. The picture of the restless discontent of modern life (1053-1094) is a commonplace of Hellenistic thought, and the range of observations in 3.830-1094 seems rooted in the more general experience of life in the new-style cities of the Hellenistic world and so specific neither to Rome nor to the world of the older civic communities. The origin of the section on Acheron (978-1023) is to be sought through earlier Epicurean and Platonic writing ultimately in the end of *Odyssey* 11. It describes a universal condition of mankind, certainly not one peculiar to Rome, although, since it is a universal condition, it is therefore true also of Rome. There are portions of the close of Book 3, however, which do breathe the atmosphere of the Late Republic. The section on Sisyphus as a symbol of the pattern of oligarchy, cast in the vocabulary of Roman public life, has been mentioned already. It is here that *imperium* is emptied of content (998). Special to Rome too are verses 1025-1035 and their examples drawn from Roman history: Ancus, Scipio, the war with Carthage. All the power and glory of the kings and great leaders of the civic past were delusions in the face of the ineluctable reality of death, which is nothing to fear, a point made more implicitly but at greater length in the description of the Athenian Plague.

The criticisms applicable to Roman life are not limited to the old Republican ethic and metropolitan social problems. They also encompass the ideas represented by Catullus. Tityos is assigned by myth to Acheron, but the reality he has is as a name or symbol for a category of human experience, in this case the passion of love. He represents the man "in amore iacentem" (992) whom "scindunt cuppedine curae" (994). The reference is not specific to Catullus and will include all such people everywhere, plentifully exemplified in Hellenistic literature, such as the poems of Philodemus, but it includes Catullus also, as the representative of a contemporary theory of value.

The position of Catullus is handled much more extensively in the diatribe against love at the end of Book 4 (verses 1058-1287), especially verses 1153-1191.[41] In the first part of this passage, the dichotomy

---

[41] See Kenney, "Doctus Lucretius" (above, note 20), 380-390.

between words and things, lovers' language and things as they are, is the subject. This is the Platonic variation on that theme,[42] something Lucretius may have gotten directly from Plato or intermediately from Epicurus. The gap between representation and reality is as great for those who set up the passion of love as the end of life as for those who aim at the glories of citizenship. *Amor* as ultimate value (*summum bonum*) rests on no better an account of the world than *civitas*, and incorporates no stronger a standard of truth. We cannot help but think of Catullus here, although the passage begins in Plato, the language is Greek, and there is nothing in it, initially, directly reminiscent of Catullus. If anything in the passage comes from the world of poetry, it seems to stem from Hellenistic epigram and speak the language of the poems of Philodemus. It is easy to believe that Lucretius had little use for this Garden schoolman who lived in comfort with so apparently vast a gap between the pretensions of his austere technical treatises in the tradition of the Founder, on the one hand, and, on the other, both the pattern of his dance of attendance on the oligarchic princes of Republican empire and the monuments to triviality in his easy-going epigrammatic celebrations of the fluctuations of common passion.[43]

The Greek of these verses will suggest the literature of Greece and, if allowed contemporary application, the literature of the Greeks in Late Republican Italy, but there is at least one phrase that may point directly to Catullus: "tota merum sal" (1162). Here we can think readily of Poem 86, in which Catullus distinguishes between the qualities attributed to Quintia and the true requirements of the adjective *formosa*, which can be applied to Lesbia alone, high among which is possession of *sal*. The quality of *sal* is a recurring theme in Catullus, as is the character of the person truly worthy of love, the subject of Poem 6. It must be admitted, however, that Catullus is concerned throughout his poems with a firm relation between words and things in poetry and love, as well as in the world of civic life (e.g., Poem 29). In the case of Suffenus (Poem 22), there is a split between poetic and personal style. In Poems 6 and 86, the one truly worthy of love or praise must reflect in her inner character the same qualities shown in physical appearance. It is because Flavius knows this (in Poem 6) that he wants to hide his girlfriend. The same point is made in Poems 41 and 43 about the mistress of Mamurra (called Ameana in our modern texts). On this ground, then, if Lucretius' target is

---

[42] Plato, *Rep.* 474d-475a.

[43] On the identification of Philodemus the philosopher and Philodemus the poet, which hardly seems a subject for productive doubt, see A. S. F. Gow and D. L. Page, *The Greek Anthology* (Cambridge 1968) 2.371-374 and on Poem XXIII (393); C. L. Neudling, *A Prosopography to Catullus* (Oxford 1955) 42-45, 123, and 137-141; DeLacy (above, note 11).

Catullus, the criticism is unfair. On the other hand, the general proposition of the diatribe in Book 4 that true value cannot be located in passion and the relationships founded on passion (where Catullus places *fides*, *amicitia*, and *pietas*) is a response to the values found in Catullus' poems. In this light, the plight of the *exclusus amator* in verses 1177-1191 may remind us of Poem 67 or perhaps Poems 32 or 51, as well as the general world of the Catullan pattern of life.[44]

The longest treatment of the civic system occurs in the history of the rise of civilization in Book 5 (verses 772-1457). This narrative should be juxtaposed to Cicero's record of the development of Rome in the *De Re Publica*, in which exactly opposite conclusions are reached about the value of human society as it developed historically and the origin of vices and evils. The development of civic society has, for Lucretius, removed man progressively farther from reality by adding to the false notions of the way the world works certain concepts, practices, institutions, and temptations that were not present to primitive man, who, of course, had his own misconceptions and troubles.[45] The developed form of society, as man has swerved more and more from clear understanding because of successive layers of false interpretation and intervening institutions, has perpetuated and multiplied the ways in which truth is concealed from him. The civic experience that for Cicero is the test of truth and the visible reflection of the real structure of the world is for Lucretius a veil, a snare, a delusion, the firm fossilization of error.

---

[44] It may be noted here, in connection with Catullus above, the attitude of Lucretius, and all that is to be said below about the place of Lucretius and Catullus in the crisis, that the Epicureans opposed ἔρως and φιλία, while Catullus linked *amor* and *amicitia*, perhaps influenced by etymology. See Rist (above, note 22) 127-139, especially 127-129. This will be a clear divergence of Catullus from Epicureanism.

[45] See Furley (above, note 21), for full discussion of this section of the poem. While each stage of human history exhibits its own evils and misconceptions, and so, as Furley notes (9-10), the issue of progress or decline is strictly irrelevant to Lucretius' presentation, as society develops more institutions, instruments, practices, and resources based on misinterpretation of nature or providing wider field for misinterpretation, it must, therefore, by devising more wrongly-based activities and values, have erected more barriers to understanding, thereby removing man further from nature. This is an intellectual rather than a moral issue. Modern man does not necessarily behave worse than primitive man, and he has created some instruments for controlling evil behavior, but his life is more distant from nature. See P. H. DeLacy, "Process and Value: An Epicurean Dilemma", *TAPA* 88 (1957) 114-126, for what might be conceived as a difficulty for Lucretius, in an Epicurean framework, perhaps caused by a conflict in the views of the Founder himself, in recounting the development of civilization. Perhaps the difficulties we perceive in Book 5 (and elsewhere) stem often from Lucretius' limitations as an original analytic thinker, from tensions in Epicurean thought he was not capable of resolving, but which he was brilliantly capable of representing, perhaps without fully realizing it. See, e.g., D. J. Furley, *Two Studies in the Greek Atomists* (Princeton 1967) 41.

Lucretius returns to the relationship of names and things (*nomina rerum*) at 5.1028-1090. The origin of names is not found in a natural relation between word and thing or in the activity of a linguistic legislator but in the interrelationship of *natura* (1028), *utilitas* (1029), and *sensus* (1058, 1087). The importance of this point of view is that the growth of language is according to nature, but the absence of a natural *relation* and an original all-knowing legislator, and the role of *utilitas* and *sensus*, allows language to be reformed and the meanings of *nomina* refashioned in accordance with a better interpretation of *sensus* and thus an alteration in the pressure of *utilitas*. The conventionality of the *nomina* themselves, their instrumental status, makes them particularly susceptible to reforms of knowledge and so sanctions Lucretius' linguistic activity in the *De Rerum Natura*.

The mythological account of the world is again allowed to act as its own refutation (878-924) in the stories of the Centaurs, Scylla, and the Chimaera. The argument that such creatures could have arisen during the earth's youth is dismissed as a reliance ''in hoc uno novitatis nomine inani'' (909), an argument from an empty name or unjustified category alone, not by reasoning from a true analysis of the world of nature by understanding things unseen on the basis of things seen.

Lucretius begins his narration of the rise of civil society at 1105 with the origin of monarchy. This history is universal in source and application, but it does provide the foundation for specific criticism of *civitas Romana*. The general history is brought home to Rome by the frequent recurrence of the Roman civic categories as targets of ridicule or revision and of the theme of *religio*: ''ad summum succedere honorem'' (1123), ''regere imperio res'' (1130), ''imperium'' (1142), ''magistratum'' (1143), ''communia foedera pacis'' (1155), ''sollemnia sacra'' (1163), ''pietas'' (1198), ''induperatorem classis'' (1227), ''divum pacem'' (1229), ''pulchros fascis saevasque securis'' (1234), ''purpurea'' (1428), ''plebeia'' (1429), ''auxilia ac socios iam pacto foedere habebant'' (1443). As described above, the civil satire culminates in the revised evaluation of Athens' contributions in the proem to Book 6 and the satire on civil helplessness which is that book's close.

Since what Lucretius says contradicts so flatly what his audience believes its experience to have been and what it considers to be the reasonable conclusions from that experience, the ground of this new interpretation and the link between experience and observation must be made ostentatious. He must make his audience agree that it does see what he sees and then find a way of winning it to the notion that there is an iron chain linking observation, idea, and action, so that conclusions become inevitable obligations, not matters of choice. This is the service performed by his formulaic style,[46] which emerges from his metrical form of expression and recalls the ancient manner of narrative literature, as well as the feelings and sense of grandeur his audience attached to that literature.

At the beginning of his verses, as a regular rhythm of sound, idea, and argument, he stabilizes certain phrases and verbal nuclei that put on display the structure of his reasoning: "nunc age", "principio", "propterea quia", "praeterea", "quapropter", "quod superest", "deinde quod usque adeo", "iamne vides igitur", "quare etiam atque etiam", "sed magis", for example. Only a reading of the poem at a stretch can evaluate the effect of this. The unrolling of the presentation of nature is blocked out in a steady form and rhythm, so that the reader begins to feel it as a shape, and a rhythm, to sense reasoning itself as physical form and movement, as something of art. The poem conveys thereby a sense of rightness and inevitability in the narration of reality that is not simply rhetorically effective but becomes eventually positively astounding in its emotional sway. The reader begins to feel persuaded, whether he is convinced or not, to believe this is the way things are. The waves of assertion become tides of plausibility. A new sense of order, based on a new poetic vocabulary, a newly and unusually poeticized vocabulary, emerges as the structure of feeling as well as of thought for this new world. The formulas for order at the beginnings of the verses are partnered by the formulas for truth, reality, appearance, and compulsion at the ends. The allowable forms of *video* occur 229 out of 256 times at the end of a verse. Combinations involving "rerum/rebus", "inane/inani", "semina", "corpora", "primordia", and "exordia" close the verse regularly and frequently. "Materiai" always does so, and "voluptas" 18 out of 21 times. "Ratione" also appears regularly in formulas for closing a verse. Perhaps the most striking of these formulas, however, are those constructed around "necessest", which ends 96 verses, out of its 105 occurrences. Compulsion arises when the close observation of the substance of reality is guided by the true method of interpretation. It is not fitting or seemly (*decet*) that we draw certain conclusions. That would be the method of civic reason, in which correct outward behavior on purely social standards is the central consideration. Lucretius is not after social appearances, but the use of natural appearances to give real understanding for ordering inward disposition. It is also not our duty (*oportet*) to draw these conclusions. This

---

[46] See J. D. Minyard (above, note 18) for a complete description of Lucretian formulas and their function, as well as a discussion of the implications of this style for understanding this poet's poem.

is a consideration based on the standard of civic *virtus*. It is the ineluctable power of reality itself, when once it has been observed and understood, that compels us to draw these conclusions. This is a requirement of perception and reason, which leaves no choice because the facts admit of no other genuine solution.

The Lucretian style creates its own new poetic order to give a feeling of order to the Epicurean explanation of the world, to develop a new lexicon of poetic reference and grammar of imagery, and to attach the force of rhetoric and literary association to Epicurean observation and analysis, to make out of this observation and analysis a new kind of narrative. The attachment of a feeling to Epicurean description and the revision of feeling about the inherited *res publica* is a necessary part of weening a non-philosophical audience from the old ideas and fixing them to the new. It requires poetry or rhetoric, not logic, because analysis can only convince. It cannot persuade. It cannot make people want to change. Only supplanting their emotional attachment to the old order by a stronger and better attachment to the new, and, if possible, detaching them from the old by making them feel toward it as they do their enemies, can accomplish this. This is the point and purpose of Lucretius' Epicurean poem: (1) the Epicurean content provides the foundation for making the criticism of civic virtue provoked by modern historical circumstance substantive, systematic, and purposive; (2) the poetic technique and form assimilates Epicureanism to inherited forms of feeling to wed a positive feeling to philosophy and detach from the inherited community the inherited feelings which were its mainstay.

The description of the relationship of style, structure, form, and purpose leads us to the conclusive sense of wholeness in the *De Rerum Natura*. Wherever we begin, whether from observation of nature, which, interpreted through the canonic, leads us to certain judgments on civic life, or from observation of civic life, whose inadequacies lead us to questions about the structure of nature, which is then to be interpreted by the combination of observation and rule, from that beginning we are led to the same conclusions, the same conclusions about physics and politics. We cannot accept the old account of reality and, therefore, we cannot accept the practice of civic virtue. Or, we see that civic virtue leads to misery, and, therefore, we are led to believe that reality must be different from the account of it which has been handed down to us. The wholeness reflects the wholeness of the original philosophy, but it is created and evaluated, shaped for feeling, by the wholeness in the form of the poem, which Lucretius makes the physical manifestation of that intellectual and emotional wholeness.

In such considerations we have the explanation of the importance of the satires on civic life to the whole poem.[47] It cannot work without them. Without them, it cannot function as both a true poem and a true representation of the Epicurean sensibility. It is the creation of this consistent sensibility, linking physics to civil satire, that is ultimately the most powerful mechanism of subtle persuasion in the poem. In this respect, Lucretius shows his understanding, conscious or not, of a great historical and psychological truth: ideas lead to thought, they do not begin in thought. They begin in feeling: the feelings which are our immediate and instinctive evaluations of our experience of the world. Lucretius' advocacy of the sufficiency of a rationalistic foundation for life rests on his sense of the emotional foundation of rationalism. In his vast appreciation of this fact of human nature, Lucretius shows the same understanding of the roots of intellectual life as Cicero and Catullus. All three point up what may have been the limit of Caesar's genius and a fundamental inner cause of his ruin, a limitation Augustus did not share.

In writing the *De Rerum Natura*, Lucretius was not simply unrolling his enthusiasm for a philosophy which, for some unaccounted and on the evidence unaccountable reason, was appealing to him personally. It may be true, ought certainly to have been true, that his personality was the sort to be attracted to Epicurus' sort of philosophy. But that is hardly interesting, and it is not significant. What is both interesting and significant are the implications of the event of this poem. That it is a poem is itself an event. It is not a poem due to a personal interest in Epicureanism. A merely personal interest in Epicureanism, if it perchance led to writing, would have led naturally to the usual kind of Epicurean writing. There is clearly something much more going on, something impersonal and highly intellectual. The *De Rerum Natura* is meant to be a service to the redefined *communis salus* of the Roman world. It rejects the Caesarian notion that there is no such thing except as it exists as a function of Caesarian ambition. It rejects the Catullan notion that real *salus* is purely emotional. And it rejects the Ciceronian idea that the reality of *communis salus* is to be located in the intellectual order of the *mos maiorum* as enriched by the compatible discoveries of Greek

---

[47] See Kenney, *Lucretius: De Rerum Natura Book III* (above, note 33) 9-12. There is more ethical poetry in Lucretius than Kenney's description may be taken to imply, as his own treatment of Lucretian satire (17-20) should indicate. Ethical poetry was entirely possible, as the satiric tradition shows, and, contrary to the claim (10n.1) that Lucretius has reversed the traditional Epicurean subordination of Canonics and Physics to Ethics, the aim of the present essay is to show that the *De Rerum Natura* preserves the Epicurean hierarchy of philosophic parts and that the aim of the poem, in structure as well as thought, is relentlessly ethical. Lucretius, read closely, can be seen to insist on this nearly everywhere.

philosophy. *Communis salus* is to be located in the framework of *voluptas*, *amicitia*, *pietas*, *fides*, and *pax* (*hominum divumque*) in their Epicurean definitions, and in the riddance from our minds of civil *religio*, *imperium*, *ius*, and *virtus*. The *De Rerum Natura* is designed as a tract for its times. This is the key to its purpose, form, structure, and role, which gained their definition from the world in and for which it was composed. Cicero, Caesar, and Catullus will have understood it, because it lives in their intellectual world. We cannot understand it, unless we understand that world and the languages it spoke.

8. *The Consequences of Crisis*

The poems of Catullus mean that for human beings ultimate reality consists of private human relationships (or relationships between human and divine personalities) and that we can know the truth about this reality by means of personal feelings, in which resides the warrant (*fides*) of statements and claims and the test of their truthfulness. These personal feelings are evaluated on the standard of rules of style (personal and literary and usually referred to in modern discussions by the term *urbanitas*), which provides the means for converting them into true and valuable *amicitia*—or, for arbitrating between true and false assertions of *amicitia* by determining which versions are truly rooted in authentic personal feeling expressive of valuable style. The goal of life, its highest value or *summum bonum*, is *amor*. Loyalty or truthfulness to the standards of personal feeling, personal *fides*, personal *amicitia*, and *amor* constitutes *pietas*, the state and practice of pure living and devotion. Civic life is the parody and mockery of this structure of thought and value. *Iustitia* is a genuine category but was driven from earth by civil ambition.

The life and works of Cicero mean that ultimate reality is found in communal historical experience and that we can know the truth about this reality by means of the gradually developing form of *civitas* as expressed in the *res publica*. The evaluation of this experience and the rule for interpreting new experience and behavior (the civic canonic) is contained in the *mos maiorum*, which provides the framework and foundation for human association, e.g., *amicitia*. All valuable relationships are social. The goal of life is *virtus*, and loyal performance of civic duty is *pietas*. These terms are still primarily social in content, but they are semantically dynamic and have been intellectualized and, to a degree, made internal and subjective, under the influence of Greek thought. *Iustitia* is a genuine category, social in character but anchored in *natura*, observable as represented in the *mos maiorum*, thus evidence of the link between nature and the tradition, the link between *natura* and *res publica*.

Caesar's career means ultimate reality is a mechanistic world of atoms and void without divine interference which we can know through sense perceptions in which *fides* resides. The standard on which this evidence of reality is interpreted, since the world of man is social, is personal ambition. This ambition dictates that we pretend ultimate reality is found in the historical experience of *civitas Romana* and that we use its language in public discussion. If we use this language, it will appear that action and thought are anchored in the civic analysis. So, the standard of personal ambition is called *mos maiorum* and all action is described by its terms of reference (*gloria, laus, pietas, imperium, dignitas, honor*). Ambition dictates our relationships, which we call by the name *amicitia* and act as if this were the old socially oriented, rather than the new regally pointed kind of association. The goal of life is *regnum*, which we call *virtus* and talk about as if it were the civic brand of *imperium*. At most, we may appear to be aiming at a Republicanized form of divinity. Loyalty or truthfulness to this account of the world is in gaining and exercising *potentia*, which we call *pietas*. The link between reality and human action is *utilitas*, but we call it *iustitia*, a name only, but one which must be employed frequently.

The *De Rerum Natura* of Lucretius means that ultimate reality is the mechanistic world of atoms and void free from divine intervention which is known through sense perceptions interpreted according to the canonic of Epicurus. *Fides* is anchored in sense perception. The rule of interpretation Lucretius names *ratio*. This *ratio* is the foundation and framework of true personal and philosophical human relationships, called by the old, redefined name *amicitia*. The aim of life is *voluptas*, defined as sustained serenity of mind, and loyalty to its values is the new *pietas*, serene contemplation of the world as it really is. The link between reality and action is *ratio*, not *iustitia*, which has nothing to do with ultimate reality but is the name of a convention or accident of history, a function of the varying histories of different societies and is therefore anchored in a derived "reality", in, in fact, any one of a number of mistakes about reality. Knowledge of the various versions of *iustitia* may help the understanding of how human society has developed, but it will not lead to an understanding of the structure of reality or the true ends of human life.

The clash over the use of Latin had consequences of semantic dislocation and opened mechanisms for deliberate obfuscation from which neither Latin nor Roman society ever recovered fully before the end of the Classical world and the victory of Christianity over both Rome and its language. It resulted eventually in a permanent gap and intellectually debilitating tension between appearance and reality caused by the persistent and deliberate application of oligarchic analysis to monarchical reality, of the language of the ancestral community to the world and institutions of cosmopolitan empire, which went far to empty the Classical forms of culture of intellectual seriousness and utility. To take only those writings of immediate political significance, it resulted also in the variety of famous attempts to surmount the corruption of public language, from the ostentatious idiosyncracy and flamboyant inversions of Persius to the hysterical marshalling of Republican imagery and feeling in Lucan, to the radically non-oligarchic and cosmopolitan unrootedness of the style of Petronius, to the austere and relentlessly intellectual refashioning of oligarchic language into an impersonal instrument of critical political analysis by Tacitus.[48]

More immediately, the crisis provoked several other consequences. Cicero had read the *De Rerum Natura* and had specific reactions to it, including his perception of the untutored native talent (*ingenium*) and the evidence of learned poetic craft (*ars*) it revealed, which he was prepared to discuss with his brother, Quintus, who had also read it in Caesar's camp, presumably as part of the Epicurean fashion there, and who likewise had made comments on its quality, apparently concentrating on the poet's *ingenium*. (*Ad Q.fr.* 2.9.3.) Cicero's reading of the poem (provoked perhaps by the recommendation of his brother or Atticus' recommendation to both), his interest in literature, his friendly relations with a number of Epicureans, including his intimate friendship with Atticus, who was a publisher, his refusal to associate Lucretius with official Epicureanism (likely thinking of him always as a poet, not an analytic philosopher), and

---

[48] See Starr (above, note 7) 203-277 and, for a somewhat different view, but one which has many important points of contact with that expressed here, Cochrane (above, note 7) 114-176. Syme, *Roman Revolution* (above, note 7) offers a famous judgment (7): "In all ages, whatever the form and name of government, be it monarchy, republic, or democracy, an oligarchy lurks behind the facade; and Roman history, Republican or Imperial, is the history of the governing class." No. The transmutation of the old into the new Rome, in which the reign of Augustus was a transitional period, encompasses the metamorphosis of oligarchy into bureaucracy. There is a difference between an oligarchy and an elite or bureaucratic class. Oligarchs rule. Bureaucrats administer, even when they make policy. The question is the source of power, and the power of an elite class is a derived not an original power. The failure of Latin to admit the consequences of political metamorphosis, the refusal even to admit the transformation, was one cause of the great tension and eventual intellectual malaise of the High Empire. Consider, for example, the importance of the theme of appearance and reality, words and things, in Tacitus: "speciosa verbis, re inania aut subdola, quantoque maiore libertatis imagine tegebantur, tanto eruptura ad infensius servitium" (*Ann.* 1.81), on the first *comitia consularia* under Tiberius; "Lepidi atque Antonii arma in Augustum cessere, qui cuncta discordiis civilibus fessa nomine principis sub imperium accepit" (*Ann.* 1.1); "dicebatur contra: pietatem erga parentem et tempora rei publicae obtentu sumpta" and "sed Pompeium imagine pacis, sed Lepidum specie amicitiae deceptos" (*Ann.* 1.10); "nomen patris patriae Tiberius...repudiavit; ...non tamen ideo faciebat fidem civilis animi; nam legem maiestatis reduxerat, cui nomen apud veteres idem, sed alia in iudicium veniebant...: facta arguebantur, dicta inpune erant. primus Augustus cognitionem de famosis libellis specie legis eius tractavit..." (*Ann.* 1.72). See also Wirszubski (above, note 7) 124-171.

his vast knowledge of Greek philosophy make plausible beyond reasonable doubt Jerome's statement that he had surveyed a fair copy of the poem as a kind of scholarly and literary proofreader to purify it of error in production.[49] This was surely at the request of Atticus, whose standards as a publisher, interest in the subject, and respect for Cicero's learning would have more than sufficed to bring the document and the man together, perhaps for the kind of oligarchic imprimatur he as a businessman would surely have liked to have had for this publication. He was offering the world not the typical pedestrian Epicurean essay or the mediocrity of the Empedoclean collections of Sallustius, but an exciting new poem, addressed to a noble audience, in the publication of which the great orator, essayist, critic, and representative of the poetic High Hellenism through his own *Aratea* had had a hand and the quality of which this expert in philosophy and literature had certified. We know Cicero read the poem and had an opinion of it. We know Jerome says he intervened in its publication (*emendavit*). We also know everything else relevant to the point of Cicero's interests, tastes, conceits, qualifications, and connections that makes his participation understandable and likely. We do not *know* anything against his participation. That is speculation, and speculation only. Given the evidence and the smallness of the oligarchic set, there is no reason to doubt that what Jerome said was true, true in the way he said it.

It is easy, in the large frame of the modern world, to forget that the Roman oligarchy, no matter how imperial and farflung its interests, how wide its power, how cosmopolitan its nature, was essentially a small town.[50] The class did not consist of many people, and these knew all

---

[49] See also M. F. Smith (above, note 18) xi-xiv, for discussion of the meaning of Jerome's statement and a different point of view; also Kenney, *Lucretius* (above, note 18) 9, again for difference of opinion. The view expressed here is strongly in disagreement with their, and, it must be said, the general modern opinion. Cicero's hostility to Epicureanism will have had little to do with a favor to a friend, a friend who was himself an Epicurean, or with his interest in poetry. He was not hostile to individual Epicureans. And consider how delicious a rebuke to Epicurean thought about poetry and what in Cicero's view was the lack of culture in the Latin Epicurean treatises publication of the *De Rerum Natura* would have been. Cicero has Torquatus say (*Fin.* 1.72, quoted above, note 36) that reading poetry, which Cicero is encouraging him to do, is a waste of time because it can contain no *solida utilitas*. Is not Lucretius' poem a refutation of that view on grounds the Epicureans would have to grant? Here is the proof that, even for Epicureans, poetry can have value, and Cicero did allow value to Lucretius' poem, both *ars* and *ingenium*.

[50] See Palmer (above, note 10) 212: "The principles of oligarchic rule were derived from a relatively closed group of habitually governing clans. The oligarchs expected their inferiors to know their place, and, above all, expected each other to know the limits set for oligarchs." Discussion also in, e.g., Syme, *Roman Revolution* (above, note 7) 10-27, 57-59, and D. Earl, *The Moral and Political Tradition of Rome* (above, note 7) 11-16. For direct connections between oligarchy and literature, see the essays by Gordon Williams and T. P. Wiseman in B. K. Gold (above, note 25).

about each other. The letters of Cicero and poems of Catullus are not simply evidence of that for which evidence is scarcely needed, but these pieces cannot be understood rightly unless we keep in mind the narrow circumstance of the class world from which they emerged.

We often say that we know little of Lucretius' life and that he seems isolated from his contemporaries because there is so little mention of him. This is an illusion born of the fact that Catullus' poems, because of their genre, mention so many people. Who mentions Catullus? Not Cicero. And Cicero speaks of Lucretius. Cornelius Nepos did, in the same sentence in which he also mentioned Lucretius, in his life of Atticus (12.4). The statement, linking the reputations of Cornelius, Lucretius, Catullus, and Atticus, and identifying Catullus and Lucretius in association with each other as the representative poets of their generation, is at once testimony to the intimacy of the class, indirect evidence for that closeness of association that allows us to argue for Ciceronian involvement in the publication of the *De Rerum Natura*, and additional argument for the thesis of this essay that the authors of the Late Republic were participants in a close communal dialogue over the intellectual fate of their class inheritance.

Cornelius (to whom Catullus dedicated his *libellus*), Catullus, and Lucretius come together in the life of Atticus. Catullus addressed Cicero in a poem, as he also addressed Memmius, under whom he served in Bithynia, in several, the same Memmius to whom Lucretius addressed his poem and Cicero later sent a letter pleading for the preservation of Epicurus' house (*Ad Fam.* 13.1). Cicero had connections with Epicureans and knew Philodemus, client of the Piso to whom Catullus refers in his poems, whom Cicero attacked in a famous speech, and who was Caesar's father-in-law. This Philodemus is certainly the Socration of Catullus' Poem 47. Catullus knew Caesar, to whom he addressed poems, who was his father's guest in Verona, and who was mightily offended by Catullus' poems about him, the Caesar with whom Cicero dealt all his civil life.[51] The possible stylistic links of Catullus, Lucretius, and Cicero to each other have been investigated frequently.[52]

This interweaving could provide a long passtime, involving Calvus, Cinna, Caelius, Clodia, Clodius, Hortensius, and others, but the picture

---

[51] Suetonius, *Julius* 73.

[52] See, e.g., H. A. J. Munro, *T. Lucreti Cari De Rerum Natura Libri Sex* (4th ed.; Cambridge 1893) on 3.57; W. A. Merrill, *Lucretius and Cicero's Verse*, UCPCP 5 (1921) 143-154; the same, "The Metrical Technique of Lucretius and Cicero", *ibid.* 7 (1924) 293-306; L. Herrmann, "Catulle et Lucrèce", *Latomus* 15 (1956) 465-480 and "Lucrèce et les amours de Catulle", *Studi Castiglioni* (Firenze 1960) 445-450.

of this world is clear.[53] Its structure of relationships eliminated the distinctions between public and private. Everything the oligarchs did was both. Withdrawal or non-participation was a gesture as public as it was private. The pressure this intimacy put on thought was enormous. The difficulty of fashioning the severely restricted Latin language for the expression of new ideas and structures of value in such a restricted social setting, where automatic and traditional controls were so deep, effective, and immediate, was extraordinary and nearly unimagineable to us. Every new linguistic gesture was potentially ominous and pregnant of possibly irredeemable confusion. Everyone knew what everyone else was saying and writing, and it was not simply natural to respond, it was impossible not to. Everything said was a response to everything else, because the language was the community property of a very small group, and even ignoring a statement was response.[54]

Cicero's reading of the *De Rerum Natura* looks like a good candidate for the immediate intellectual cause of his *De Re Publica* and, later, *De Legibus*. He had read Lucretius' poem by February of 54 B.C., perhaps some months earlier, and he began work on the *De Re Publica* the next May.[55] The *De Legibus*, begun a couple of years later, is a pendant to the earlier treatise. The other great works of Cicero's career as a philosophical essayist, as the evaluator of Greek thought on the standard of the *mos maiorum*, come next. They are the product of the last and severest decade of the crisis, following the turmoil of the 50's, its riots, exile, postponed elections, and assassinations, following Catullus and Lucretius, composed in the face of the violent challenge of real civil war and the new-style autocracy of Caesar. In these works, as in these years of the crisis, Epicureanism played a mighty part.

The *De Rerum Natura* will have been a great provocation to Cicero, whose whole life is witness to his understanding of the consequences of poetry in civic life and the varying ethics of the different genres. He could now see how far Epicureanism might go. Not only in the Italian towns, not only among his more serious friends and acquaintances, and not only in the shape of the parlor Epicureanism of the fancy salons of Piso and his like, but now, at the heart of the Roman cultural accomplishment, the Garden was making its way and showing profound potential for subver-

---

[53] See C. L. Neudling (above, note 43), especially the articles on Asinius Pollio, Caelius Rufus, Piso, Cornelius Nepos, Cinna, Hortensius, Caesar, Lesbia, Lesbius, Calvus, Mamurra, Torquatus, Memmius, Philodemus, Pompey, Cicero, Vatinius.

[54] Compare Rubino (above, note 13) 293, and D. Earl, *The Moral and Political Tradition of Rome* (above, note 7) 11-43.

[55] Cicero, *Ad Q.fr.* 2.10(9).3 (February 54 B.C.), on Lucretius; *Ad Q.fr.* 2.13(12) (May 54 B.C.) and 3.5 (October or November 54 B.C.), on the *De Re Publica*.

sion. No longer confined to the clumsy and unrefined prose renditions of strict doctrine, Epicureanism, quite unexpectedly, now had a big Latin poem to its credit, one that took on the entire literary as well as constitutional heritage of Rome, one that sought to change the nature of literature as well as everything else. It was a poem both epic and philosophical, the kind of poem Cicero took most seriously and thought ought to be taken very seriously. And it was the best long poem in Latin yet. This was more trouble than anything alien had been at Rome, and, as he looked around, Cicero could see that it was only part of a seething cauldron. The political crisis, of which Cicero had long been aware and with which he had spent his life dealing, was now, more than ever before, a fully intellectual crisis as well. No longer could Epicureanism simply provide convenient material for forensic satire directed at opponents like Piso, an instrument of party fun and frolic. It was a real enemy now, and for the next ten years Cicero dismantled it in essay after essay, spending as much time erecting intellectual barriers against it and entrenching the constitutional patrimony in fortifications of sophisticated intellectual analysis as he did finessing Caesar, engaging in mortal combat with Antony, and attempting to hold up *res publica* virtually by the scruff of its battered neck.

Ironically, Epicureanism took another surprising turn in 44 B.C.[56] It was shocked out of its fascination with Caesar and took up the colors of the opposition. For what reason? Among whatever others, surely because it saw through at last the veils of his seducing rationalism to the moral nihilism at the center of his policy. The kind of thinking exhibited by his cosmopolitan reforms (institutional and calendrical), the contempt for superstition, and the understanding of atomism had long worked to charm the Gardeners into thinking him one of themselves at heart. But the thoroughly autocratic ambition, which was becoming more apparent, and, much more to the point, the religious manipulations, the arrangement of religous forms for autocratic purposes, must have come, when the realization of Caesar's true character set finally in, like a thunderbolt. The jolt set the sectarians loose from their delusive addiction, and the conversion of Cassius became then not the confirmation of a Caesarian loyalty but an addition to the resources of conspiracy, so that Epicureans and Stoics joined causes with unphilosophic Republicans in the momentary requirement of cutting the Caesarian cancer out of their world.

The assassination of Caesar was one of the responses to the crisis, an answer supported by the proponents of all the other solutions, but it did

---

[56] A. Momigliano (above, note 11) 151-157.

not take. In fact, Caesarism—not Ciceronianism, Catonism, Pompey-
ism, Catullanism, nor Epicureanism—was the final and real answer,
political and intellectual, to the crisis of the Late Republic. This was clear
after a dozen more years of civil disruption. What that answer entailed in
the end was the linguistic nihilism mentioned above, the nihilism at the
center of the Caesarian brand of politics.

It entailed much else, however, much else that, however great the
Augustan trickery, was of considerable cultural worth and eventual importance for the intellectual content of Western civilization. The public
or advertized solution of crisis was the Ciceronian evaluation. This is,
essentially, what we find worked out in Augustan propaganda and in the
poems of Virgil and Horace. In the poems, it is complex and even ambiguous, but the attitude of the poets is rooted in the Ciceronian
adherence to the values of the *mos maiorum*, a Ciceronian richness of
Hellenic culture, and a Ciceronian adroitness in the balance of historical
gain and loss, never allowing the loss to be forgotten in the contemplation
of gain, but never allowing the acknowledgement and acceptance of gain
to be made forfeit by the useless worship of loss.

When the Epicureans executed their sedition from Caesar, surely this
was the point and cause of the Virgilian abandonment of his Epicurean
affection.[57] In the moment of decision, Virgil weighed chances (the
chances of history, not of personal fortune) and decided he was more
Caesarian than schoolman, and so he stayed the course with Octavian
and Maecenas. Always sophisticated and complicated, he never forgot
his Neapolitan lessons and always allowed the influence of Lucretius on
his sensibility and morality its due in his style, imagery, and judgment.
His Caesarian adherency was never such that he surrendered his moral
independence or failed to acknowledge Caesarism's darker side and
danger. This is clear in the *Eclogues* (as in 1, 9, and 10) and throughout
the *Aeneid*, including its end, where the un-Epicurean and un-Stoic *furor*
finally overcomes Aeneas to his moral discredit.[58] Virgil does not allow
his *Aeneid* the calm resolution of reconciliation his readers had found in
the *Iliad*, the *Odyssey*, or the *Oresteia*. His Epicureanism must have had effect here, and perhaps also the suddenness, the violence, and the
darkness of the ending of the *De Rerum Natura* as it had been left to him.

On the other side, so much of what Virgil accomplishes is an open rejection of Lucretius and Epicureanism. In Eclogue 1, the "deus ille fuit,
deus, inclute Memmi" of *De Rerum Natura* 5.8 is answered by Tityrus'

---

[57] On Virgil's connection with Epicureanism, see: N. W. DeWitt, *Virgil's Biographia
Litteraria* (London 1923) 36-46, and T. Frank, *Vergil: A Biography* (Oxford 1922) 47-109.

[58] See M. C. J. Putnam, *Virgil's Pastoral Art* (Princeton 1970) 20-81 and 293-394 and
The Poetry of the Aeneid (Cambridge, Mass. 1965) 151-201.

"deus nobis haec otia fecit / namque erit ille mihi semper deus" (6-7). This declaration is, of course, strongly qualified by the picture of Meliboeus' situation, and the other ambiguities of the poem, but Virgil has moved away from Lucretius and, with whatever qualification, come down on the other side.

The full extent of Virgil's Epicurean apostasy, with its qualifications, is of course set out in the *Aeneid*. Here Virgil became what Lucretius had wanted to become, the spring of a new literature and the school-book of Rome. But his sources and models were Rome, history, and Aeneas, not Athens, philosophy, and Epicurus. As Lucretius began his poem with "Aeneadum genetrix", so Virgil writes his about Aeneas and his mother Venus, not reinterpreted on philosophical lines but with their traditional and historical force. Whereas Lucretius' poem ignored *virtus* and offered solutions to violence, Virgil's poem was a poem about "arma virumque". The Virgilian tragic view of violence, learned from Epicureanism, is well known, but he also believed that, whatever its cost, sometimes the only road to gain, forced by an inelecutable concatenation of historical circumstances, was the road of war.

Virgil's poem was a Ciceronian account of the origin of Rome and the foundations of the *mos maiorum*, not the Lucretian satiric anthropology. It was a celebration of *pius Aeneas* (and *fidus Achates*) for *virtus, fides, dignitas, gloria* in his struggle to found a city which would have everlasting *imperium*. It is a poem founded in *ius*, not *ratio*, whose core is the intervention of the gods in human affairs, not their indifference, the worth of *religio*, not its noxious vanity, the necessity of the traditional *pax deorum*, not a new conception, and the longest and most elaborate picture of reward and punishment in the Underworld we have from Classical poetry, not the rejection of the world of Acheron as the product of a silly and morally debilitating *religio*. And, queen of ironies, when Dido, caught in her uncivil and un-Epicurean *furor* for Aeneas, scorns his allegation of religious motivation for abandoning her to fulfill his obligation to Rome's destiny, she reasons her case straight on the line of the *ratio Epicuri Lucretique*: "scilicet is superis labor est, ea cura quietos / sollicitat" (4.379-380). Dido is hardly the princess of Epicurean pleasure, but her satire is Lucretian in its tone and force, and she is wrong. Aeneas is right, as we know, as Virgil tells us: the gods have intervened, this is their *labor*, and they told him to go to Italy and Rome's future.

The mission of the *Aeneid* is the rehabilitation of every category devastated by the *De Rerum Natura*, the resurrection of the old world view, the salvation of *religio* and the *mos maiorum*. Virgil's goal is the reestablishment of the literary tradition by a demonstration of a different way of saving epic for the modern mind. Philosophy, history, rationalism can be incorporated as defenses, not substitutes, of the ancient form and content, to enrich and save its significance. His hope was to replace the best long poem in Latin, the new-style epic, the great threat to the whole range of the civic inheritance, with a better long poem, an old-style epic in a new style, to save civil value for a new age. And he succeeded, as an historical and an aesthetic fact, although the value he saved he saved only in his poem. He did not, because he could not, prove that what might be accomplished for the mind and for art was an accomplishment in the facts of life for a ruthless, intellectually vicious, and morally nihilistic absolutism. He saved Rome and civic value and moral insight for a later age, but he could not save these things for his own. He could keep a hope alive, but he could not, for himself and his fellows, make it real.

The interpretation of Augustan literature, all of it, is not complete until it takes account of it as the literature of the first post-crisis generation. It is the first generation of the attempt to put back in an absolutist framework what had been destroyed in the shredding of the structure of Republican liberty. The task was never completed, because it could not be, until the triumph of Christianity,[59] but a large number of notable and permanently valuable achievements flowed from the attempt, even more valuable in the present century of the search for dignity and a motive for action in historical terms, when the threat of political, economic, and technological absolutism has darkened beyond all possible previous imagination. It is not only in the framework of Republican crisis itself, but also in that of the reaction of the later generations of pseudo-oligarchic literature to the consequences of the crisis, faking oligarchic light because of and as relief to absolutist darkness, that the measure of Lucretius should be taken, for he occupies a place in the history of Roman intellectual life far more securely than ever he can hold his own in the world of Hellenic scholastic thought.

---

[59] See Starr (above, note 7) 278-359 and Cochrane (above, note 7).

SELECTED BIBLIOGRAPHY

All the works in the following bibliography have been cited in the notes. This bibliography does not include, however, works which were cited only incidentally, that is, those whose value is mainly illustrative or which were mentioned in discussion of points generated by but not central to the present argument. The items included are of two kinds: (1) those containing material and analyses crucial to the development of this discussion; (2) those which, while not in themselves fundamental studies, contain comprehensive bibliographies of scholarship on questions related to the background of this essay. The latter category has been especially important for keeping the notes and bibliography within manageable limits, since the number of works able to be cited for a treatment even as brief as this is very large. The record of scholarly work in books such as those by Adcock and Ogilvie, therefore, is an important addition to the bibliographical foundations of the present work, making it possible to list here primarily that material concerned with the relevant major issues of Late Republican thought. In citing ancient texts, I have used the most recent Teubner and, when such exist, Oxford editions, as well as Bailey's 1947 text, translation, and commentary for Lucretius, D. F. S. Thomson's edition (Chapel Hill 1978) for Catullus, and Shackleton-Bailey's text and translation (Cambridge 1965-1970) for Cicero's letters to Atticus.

Adcock, F. E., *Roman Political Ideas and Practice.* Ann Arbor: University of Michigan Press, 1964.

Allen, W., Jr and P. H. DeLacy, "The Patrons of Philodemus." *Classical Philology* 34 (1939) 59-65.

Badian, E., *Foreign Clientelae (264-70 B.C.).* Oxford: The Clarendon Press, 1958.

—, *Roman Imperialism in the Late Republic.* 2nd ed; repr. Ithaca: Cornell University Press, 1971.

Bailey, C., *Titi Lucreti Cari De Rerum Natura Libri Sex.* Edited with translation and commentary. 3 vols. Oxford: The Clarendon Press, 1947.

Bloch, R., *The Origins of Rome.* New York: Frederick A. Praeger, 1960.

Boyancé, P., *Lucrèce et l'epicurisme.* Paris: Presses Universitaires de France, 1963.

—, "Velatum ... ad lapidem." *Latomus* 35 (1976) 550-554.

Brunt, P. A., *Social Conflicts in the Roman Republic.* New York: W. W. Norton & Co., 1971.

Bury, J. B., *et al.*, *The Hellenistic Age.* 1923; repr. New York: W. W. Norton & Co., 1970.

Clarke, M. L., *The Roman Mind: Studies in the History of Thought from Cicero to Marcus Aurelius.* New York: W. W. Norton & Co., 1968.

Clay, D., *Lucretius and Epicurus.* Ithaca: Cornell University Press, 1983.

Cochrane, C. N., *Christianity and Classical Culture: A Study of Thought and Action from Augustus to Augustine.* Rev. ed. 1944; repr. Oxford: Oxford University Press, 1968.

Cole, T., "The Saturnian Verse." *Yale Classical Studies* 21 (1969) 1-73.

DeLacy, P. H., "Cicero's Invective Against Piso." *Transactions and Proceedings of the American Philological Association* 72 (1941) 49-58.

—, "Lucretius and the History of Epicureanism." *Transactions and Proceedings of the American Philological Association* 79 (1948) 12-23.

—, "Lucretius and Plato." Συζητησις: *Studi sull'Epicureismo greco e romano offerti a Marcello Gigante.* Naples: Macchiaroli, 1983. Pp. 291-307.

—, "Process and Value: An Epicurean Dilemma." *Transactions and Proceedings of the American Philological Association* 88 (1957) 114-126.

DeWitt, N. W., *Epicurus and His Philosophy.* Minneapolis: University of Minnesota Press, 1954.

—, *Virgil's Biographia Litteraria.* London: Humphrey Milford, Oxford University Press, 1923.

Dudley, D. R., ed., *Lucretius*. New York: Basic Books, 1965.

Earl, D., *The Moral and Political Tradition of Rome*. Ithaca: Cornell University Press, 1967.

—, *The Political Thought of Sallust*. Cambridge: The University Press, 1961.

Edelstein, L., "Primum Graius Homo (Lucretius 1.66)." *Transactions and Proceedings of the American Philological Association* 71 (1940) 78-90.

Farrington, B., *Science and Politics in the Ancient World*. New York: Oxford University Press, 1940.

—, *The Faith of Epicurus*. New York: Basic Books, 1967.

Ferrero, L., *Poetica Nuova in Lucrezio*. Firenze: La Nuova Italia, 1949.

Frank, T., *Vergil: A Biography*. Oxford: Basil Blackwell, 1922.

Furley, D. J., "Lucretius and the Stoics." *Bulletin of the Institute of Classical Studies* 13 (1966) 13-33.

—, "Lucretius the Epicurean." Entretiens sur l'antiquité classique t. 24: *Lucrèce*. Genève: Fondation Hardt, 1978. Pp. 1-37.

—, *Two Studies in the Greek Atomists*. Princeton: Princeton University Press, 1967.

Fustel de Coulanges, Numa Denis, *La Cité Antique*. 1864; repr. Paris: Hachette, 1927.

Galinsky, G. K., *Aeneas, Sicily and Rome*. Princeton: Princeton University Press, 1969.

Gelzer, M., *Caesar: Politician and Statesman*. 6th ed. trans. P. Needham. Oxford: Basil Blackwell, 1968.

—, *The Roman Nobility*. Trans. R. Seagar. Oxford: Basil Blackwell, 1969.

Gordon, A. E., "On the Origins of the Latin Alphabet: Modern Views." *California Studies in Classical Antiquity* 2 (1969) 157-170.

Gow, A. S. F. and D. L. Page, eds., *The Greek Anthology: The Garland of Philip and Some Contemporary Epigrams*. 2 vols. Cambridge: Cambridge University Press, 1968.

Grimal, P., "Le poème de Lucrèce en son temps." Entretiens sur l'antiquité classique t. 24: *Lucrèce*. Genève: Fondation Hardt, 1978. Pp. 233-270.

Harris, W. V., *War and Imperialism in Republican Rome: 327-70 B.C.* Oxford: The Clarendon Press, 1979.

Herrmann, L., "Catulle et Lucrèce." *Latomus* 15 (1976) 465-480.

—, "Lucrèce et les amours de Catulle." *Studi in onore di Luigi Castiglioni*. Firenze: Sansoni, 1960, Pp. 445-450.

Houghton, H. P., "Lucretius as Satirist." *Transactions and Proceedings of the American Philological Association* 43 (1912) xxxiv-xxxix.

Howe, H. M., "Three Groups of Roman Epicureans." *Transactions and Proceedings of the American Philological Association* 79 (1948) 341-342.

—, "Amafinius, Lucretius, and Cicero." *American Journal of Philology* 72 (1951) 57-62.

Huergon, J., *The Rise of Rome to 264 B.C.* Trans. J. Willis. London: Batsford, 1973.

Kenney, E. J., *Lucretius*. Oxford: Oxford University Press, 1977.

—, *Lucretius: De Rerum Natura Book III*. Cambridge: The University Press, 1971.

—, Review of P. H. Schrijvers, *Horror ac Divina Voluptas*. *Classical Review* 86 (1972) 348-351.

—, "Doctus Lucretius." *Mnemosyne* 23 (1970) 366-392.

Kleve, K., "The Philosophical Polemics in Lucretius." Entretiens sur l'antiquité classique t. 24: *Lucrèce*. Genève: Fondation Hardt, 1978. Pp. 39-75.

Merrill, W. A., *Lucretius and Cicero's Verse*. University of California Publications in Classical Philology, Vol. 5, No. 9, pp. 143-154. Berkeley: University of California Press, 1921.

—, *The Metrical Technique of Lucretius and Cicero*. University of California Publications in Classical Philology, Vol. 7, No. 10, pp. 293-306. Berkeley: University of California Press, 1924.

Minyard, J. D., "Critical Notes on Catullus 29." *Classical Philology* 76 (1971) 174-181.

—, *Mode and Value in the De Rerum Natura: A Study in Lucretius's Metrical Language*. Hermes Einzelschriften 39. Wiesbaden: Franz Steiner Verlag, 1978.

Momigliano, A., "An Interim Report on the Origins of Rome." *Journal of Roman Studies* 53 (1963) 95-121.

—, "The Origins of the Roman Republic." *Interpretations: Theory and Practice*. Ed. C. S. Singleton. Baltimore: The Johns Hopkins Press, 1969. Pp. 1-34.

—, Review of B. Farrington, *Science and Politics in the Ancient World*. *Journal of Roman Studies* 31 (1941) 149-157.

Morford, M. P. O., "Ancient and Modern in Cicero's Poetry." *Classical Philology* 62 (1967) 112-116.

Murley, C., "Lucretius and the History of Satire." *Transactions and Proceedings of the American Philological Association* 70 (1939) 380-395.

Murray, G., *Five Stages of Greek Religion*. 3rd ed. 1951; repr. New York: Doubleday & Co., N.D.

Neudling, C. L., *A Prosopography to Catullus*. Iowa Studies in Classical Philology. Oxford, 1955.

—, "Epicureans and the 'New Poets'." *Transactions and Proceedings of the American Philological Association* 80 (1949) 429-430.

Nichols, J. H., Jr., *Epicurean Political Philosophy*. Ithaca: Cornell University Press, 1976.

Ogilvie, R. M., *Early Rome and the Etruscans*. Atlantic Highlands, N.J.: Humanities Press, 1976.

Palmer, R. E. A., *The Archaic Community of the Romans*. Cambridge: Cambridge University Press, 1970.

—, Review of S. Weinstock, *Divus Julius*. *Athenaeum* 51 (1973) 201-213.

Putnam, M. C. J., *The Poetry of the Aeneid*. Cambridge, Mass.: Harvard University Press, 1965.

—, *Virgil's Pastoral Art*. Princeton: Princeton University Press, 1970.

Rist, J. M., *Epicurus: An Introduction*. Cambridge: Cambridge University Press, 1972.

Ross, D. O., Jr., *Style and Tradition in Catullus*. Cambridge, Mass.: Harvard University Press, 1969.

Rubino, C., "The Erotic World of Catullus." *Classical World* 68 (1974-1975) 289-298.

Sabine, S. H. and S. B. Smith., *On the Commonwealth: Marcus Tullius Cicero*. Translated, with an introduction. 1929; repr. Indianapolis: Bobbs-Merrill, N.D.

Schrijvers, P. H., *Horror ac Divina Voluptas: Études sur la poétique et la poésie de Lucrèce*. Amsterdam: Adolf M. Hakkert, 1970.

Sikes, E. E., *Lucretius: Poet and Philosopher*. Cambridge: The University Press, 1931.

Smith, M. F., *Lucretius: De Rerum Natura*. With an English translation by W. H. D. Rouse. Revised with new text, introduction, notes and index by Martin Ferguson Smith. Cambridge, Mass.: Harvard University Press, 1975.

Starr, C. G., *Civilization and the Caesars: The Intellectual Revolution in the Roman Empire*. 1954; repr. New York, W. W. Norton & Co., 1965.

Syme, R., *The Roman Revolution*. Oxford: Oxford University Press, 1939.

—, *Sallust*. Sather Classical Lectures 33. Berkeley: University of California Press, 1964.

Tait, J. I. M., *Philodemus' Influence on the Latin Poets*. Diss. Bryn Mawr, 1941.

Taylor, L. R., *Party Politics in the Age of Caesar*. Sather Classical Lectures 22. Berkeley: University of California Press, 1949.

Thornton, A., *The Living Universe: Gods and Men in Virgil's Aeneid*. Mnemosyne Supplementum 46. Leiden: E. J. Brill, 1976.

Versnel, H., *Triumphus*. Leiden: E. J. Brill, 1970.

Wagenvoort, H., *Roman Dynamism: Studies in ancient Roman thought, language, and custom*. 1947; repr. Westport, Conn.: Greenwood Press, 1976.

Walbank, F. W., *The Hellenistic World*. Cambridge: Cambridge University Press, 1982.

Wallach, B. P., *Lucretius and the Diatribe Against the Fear of Death: De Rerum Natura III 830-1094*. Mnemosyne Supplementum 40. Leiden: E. J. Brill, 1976.

Waltz, R., "Lucrèce satirique." *Lettres d'Humanité* 8 (1949) 78-103.

Waszink, J. H., *Lucretius and Poetry*. Mededelingen der Koninklijke Nederlandse Akademie van Wetenschappen, Afd. Letterkunde, 17. Amsterdam: N.V. Noord-Hollandsche Uitgevers Maatschappij, 1954.

Weinstock, S., *Divus Julius*. Oxford: The Clarendon Press, 1971.

Winspear, A. D., *Lucretius and Scientific Thought*. Montreal: Harvest House, 1963.

Wirszubski, Ch., *"Audaces*: A Study in Political Phraseology.*" Journal of Roman Studies* 51 (1961) 12-22.

—, "Cicero's *Cum Dignitate Otium*: a Reconsideration.*" Journal of Roman Studies* 44 (1954) 1-13.

—, *Libertas as a Political Idea at Rome During the Late Republic and Early Principate*. Cambridge: At the University Press, 1950.

Wiseman, T. P., *Cinna the Poet and Other Roman Essays*. Leicester: Leicester University Press, 1974.

—, *"Pete nobiles amicos*: Poets and Patrons in Late Republican Rome.*" Literary and Artistic Patronage in Ancient Rome*. Ed. B. K. Gold. Austin: University of Texas Press, 1982. Pp. 28-49.

Wistrand, E., *Caesar and Contemporary Society*. Humaniora 15. Göteborg: Kungl. Vetenskaps-och Vitterhets-Samhället, 1978.

INDEX

1. PRINCIPAL LATIN WORDS

amicitia, 19, 26, 27, 29, 36, 41, 43, 44, 49, 50, 52, 65, 70, 71, 72 n. 48
amicus, 25
amor, 26, 63, 64, 65 n. 44, 70
animus, 41, 42, 72 n. 48
audacia, 44
audeo (ausus), 24, 33 n. 17, 44
benefacta, 26, 27
beneficium, 9, 11, 12 n. 7
civitas, 2, 5, 6, 8-11, 13, 16, 17, 24, 25, 28-31, 36, 39, 40, 42, 44, 47, 48, 50-52, 55, 56 n. 34, 57, 61, 64, 66, 70, 71
classis, 11, 39, 48, 54, 66
corpus, 41, 42, 45, 54, 67
deus, 9, 41, 57, 77, 78
dignitas, 7, 8, 12, 16, 17, 23, 27, 50, 71, 78
dignus, 50
divus, 48, 60, 70
falsum, 21
fama, 41
familia, 9-11, 38, 39
fas, 9, 22, 23, 24
fides, 9, 11, 14, 20, 26-28, 31, 32, 38-42, 44, 48, 50-52, 65, 70, 71, 72 n. 48, 78
fidus, 78
foedus, 9, 26, 27, 41, 66
furor, 77, 78
gloria, 9-11, 24, 38, 54, 71, 78
honor, 9, 10, 48, 50, 54, 66, 71
imperator, 24, 25
imperium, 9, 11, 24, 48, 50, 63, 66, 70, 71, 72 n. 48, 78
impius, 36, 37, 39
inane, 41, 45, 67
ira, 19
ius, 9, 10, 12, 51, 52, 70, 78
iustitia, 25, 31, 70, 71
iustus, 9, 51
laus, 9, 11, 24, 31, 38, 59, 71
lex, 9, 31, 51, 72 n. 48
maiores, 8-9, 11, 31
materia (materies), 45, 67
mens, 41, 43, 44
mos, 60
mos maiorum, 4, 5-12, 13 n. 7, 14, 15, 16 n. 9, 20, 22, 23, 29-31, 39-44, 46, 47, 50, 55, 61, 69-71, 75, 77, 78
natura, 8, 42, 45, 50, 52, 54, 61, 66, 70
necesse, 67-68

nefas, 9
negotium, 23
nobilis, 10, 11, 25, 39, 46 n. 25
nobilitas, 9-12, 46 n. 25, 54
nomen, 50, 52, 56, 66, 72 n. 48
novitas, 43, 52, 66
novus, 43-45, 52, 53
nugae, 24
odium, 19
officium, 9, 11, 12 n. 7
otiosus, 23, 33 n. 17
otium, 23, 24
pater, 9-11, 38, 39, 50
patria, 9, 36, 50, 52, 72 n. 48
patronus, 9-11, 25
pax, 9, 59, 66, 70, 72 n. 48
Pax Augusta, 1
pax deorum (divum), 9, 20, 48, 49, 59, 66, 78
pietas, 9-12, 20, 23, 26, 27, 29, 31, 37-40, 47-50, 52, 56 n. 34, 65, 66, 70, 71, 72 n. 48
pio, 38, 39
pius, 26, 78
potentia, 71
pudicus, 26
pudor, 31, 50
purus, 26
ratio, 36, 40-42, 44, 45, 48, 50-52, 54, 56, 57, 59, 60, 67, 71, 78
regnum, 71
religio, 9, 10, 12, 13 n. 7, 17 n. 10, 20, 23, 31, 36-41, 46-50, 52-54, 56, 57, 59-61, 66, 70, 78
res, 20, 21, 27, 32, 36, 41-45, 50, 52, 54, 56, 57, 60, 66, 67, 72
res publica, 8, 11, 13 n. 7, 15, 21, 25, 28-32, 41, 68, 70, 72 n. 48, 76
rex, 38, 54
sacer, 9, 38
sal, 64
salus, 9, 26, 27, 36-38, 41, 50, 51, 69, 70
semina, 41, 45, 67
senatus, 9-11
senes, 8, 11, 23
sensus, 42, 45, 50, 66
severitas, 9, 10, 23
species, 42, 45, 54, 72 n. 48
urbanitas, 70

utilitas, 58 n. 36, 66, 71, 73 n. 49
verus, 20, 21, 36, 42
victor, 41
victoria, 41

virtus, 9-12, 30, 31, 36, 38-41, 43, 44, 51, 52, 54, 68, 70, 71, 78
voluptas, 36, 41, 43, 45, 50, 51, 52, 59, 67, 70, 71

2. MODERN SCHOLARS

Adcock, F. E., 12 n. 7
Allen, W., Jr., 18 n. 11
Badian, E. 12 n. 7
Bailey, C., 42 n. 22, 44 n. 23, 46 n. 27, 49 n. 28
Benedickston, D. T., 27 n. 13
Bevan, E., 14 n. 8
Bloch, R., 4 n. 1
Boyance, P., 33 n. 18, 49 n. 28
Brunt, P. A., 6 n. 3
Bury, J. B., 14 n. 8
Clarke, M. L., 12 n. 7, 18 n. 11
Clay, D., 33 n. 18, 34 n. 19
Cochrane, C. N., 13 n. 7, 30 n. 15, 72 n. 48
Cole, T., 4 n. 1
DeLacy, P. H., 18 n. 11, 55 n. 34, 64 n. 43, 65 n. 45
DeWitt, N. W., 17 n. 10, 18 n. 11, 49 n. 29, 52 n. 32, 58 n. 36, 77 n. 57
Dudley, D. R., 44 n. 23, 53 n. 33
Earl, D. C., 5 n. 2, 12 n. 7, 73 n. 50, 75 n. 54
Edelstein, L., 40 n. 21
Ernout, A.-A. Meillet, 9 n. 6
Farrington, B., 14 n. 8, 17 n. 10, 18 n. 11, 36 n. 20, 40 n. 21, 45 n. 25, 49 n. 29, 55 n. 34
Ferrero, L., 28 n. 14
Furley, D. J., 40 n. 21, 42 n. 22, 55 n. 34, 56 n. 35, 65 n. 45
Frank, T., 77 n. 57
Fustel de Coulanges, Numa Denis, 12 n. 7
Galinsky, G. K., 4 n. 1
Gelzer, N., 12 n. 7, 16 n. 9
Gold, B. K., 46 n. 25, 73 n. 50
Gordon, A. E., 4 n. 1
Gow, A. S. F.-D. Page, 64 n. 43
Grimal, P., 35 n. 20
Guarducci, M., 4 n. 1
Harris, W. V., 12 n. 7
Herrmann, L., 74 n. 52
Houghton, H. P., 53 n. 33
Howe, H. M., 18 n. 11
Huergon, J., 4 n. 1
Kenney, E. J., 28 n. 14, 33 n. 18, 34 n. 19, 35 n. 20, 45 n. 25, 53 n. 33, 61 n. 40, 63 n. 41, 69 n. 47, 73 n. 49
Kleve, K., 55 n. 34

Konstan, D., 12 n. 7
Lloyd-Jones, H., 8 n. 5
Maguiness, W. S., 44 n. 23
Merrill, W. A., 74 n. 52
Michels, A. K., 36 n. 20
Minyard, J. D., 24 n. 12, 27 n. 13, 33 n. 18, 59 n. 38, 67 n. 46
Momigliano, A., 4 n. 1, 17 n. 10, 18 n. 11, 76 n. 56
Morford, M. P. O., 32 n. 17, 45 n. 24
Munro, H. A. J., 74 n. 52
Murley, C., 53 n. 33
Murray, G., 14 n. 8
Neudling, C. L., 28 n. 14, 64 n. 43, 75 n. 53
Nichols, J. H., Jr., 56 n. 34
Ogilvie, R. M., 4 n. 1
Palmer, L. R., 9 n. 6
Palmer, R. E. A., 12 n. 7, 17 n. 10, 37 n. 50
Putnam, M. C. J., 77 n. 58
Rist, J. M., 42 n. 22, 49 n. 29, 51 n. 31, 52 n. 32, 65 n. 44
Ross, D. O., Jr., 27 n. 13
Rubino, C., 27 n. 13, 46 n. 26, 75 n. 54
Sabine, G. H.-S. B. Smith, 31 n. 16
Schrijvers, P. H., 33 n. 18
Segal, E., 12 n. 7
Sikes, E. E., 33 n. 18
Singleton, C. S., 4 n. 1
Smith, M. F., 33 n. 18, 73 n. 49
Starr, C. G., 13 n. 7, 32 n. 17, 72 n. 48, 79 n. 59
Syme, R., 12 n. 7, 72 n. 48, 73 n. 50
Tait, J. I. M., 28 n. 14
Taylor, L. R., 12 n. 7
Thorton, A., 13 n. 7, 55 n. 34
Versnel, H., 4 n. 1
Wagenvoort, H., 8 n. 5
Walbank, F. W., 14 n. 8
Wallach, B. P., 53 n. 33, 61 n. 40
Waltz, R., 53 n. 33
Waszink, J. H., 33 n. 18
Weinstock, S., 12 n. 7, 17 n. 10
Williams, G., 73 n. 50
Winspear, A. D., 17 n. 10, 55 n. 34
Wirszubski, Ch., 13 n. 7, 16 n. 9, 32-33 n. 17, 72 n. 48
Wiseman, T. P., 45 n. 25, 73 n. 50
Wistrand, E., 16 n. 9

3. PRINCIPAL SUBJECTS

Acheron, 49, 62, 78
Achilles, 8, 16, 38
Aeneas, 3, 38, 77, 78
Agamemnon, 37, 38
Alexandrianism, 44
alphabet, 3, 4 n. 1, 6
Aristotle, 56 n. 34
Aristotelianism, 18, 55 n. 3
Athens, 59, 60, 61, 63, 66, 78
Atticus, 28 n. 13, 32 n. 17, 72-74
Augustus (Octavian), 69, 72 n. 48, 77
Aulis, 36, 38
Caelius Rufus, 74, 75 n. 53
Caesar, C. Julius, 15-27, 29, 30, 32 n. 17, 36 n. 20, 55, 69-72, 74-77
canonic, 40, 42, 68, 69 n. 47
Cassius, 76
Catiline, 16 n. 9, 19
Cato the Elder, 31, 32
Cato the Younger, 17, 19-21, 77
Catullus, 15, 21, 22-31, 32-33 n. 17, 34, 41, 43, 44, 46, 56 n. 34, 63-65, 69, 70, 74, 75, 77
Ceres, 55, 57, 59
Cicero, M., 8 n. 4, 15, 16 n. 9, 17 n. 10, 18, 20, 22, 23, 25, 29-32, 33 n. 17, 34 n. 19, 40, 41, 44, 46, 49 n. 29, 51, 52, 54, 58 n. 36, 61, 65, 69, 70, 72-76, 78
Cicero, Q., 18, 72
Christianity, 1, 71, 79
Cornelius Nepos, 24, 28 n. 13, 74, 75 n. 53
Crassus, 15, 25, 55
Demetrius of Magnesia, 32 n. 17
Diogenes Laertius, 58 n. 36
Empedocles, 34 n. 19, 73
Ennius, 34 n. 19, 36, 43, 57
Epicureanism, 17-22, 24, 28, 29, 33, 34, 38-40, 42, 45, 46, 48, 49, 51-63, 65 n. 44, 68, 69, 72, 73, 75-78
Epicurus, 19, 22, 28, 33-36, 39, 40, 41, 42 n. 22, 50, 55-61, 64, 69, 74, 78
Etruscan, 3, 5
Greek culture and influence, 1-6, 8, 13-15, 19, 20, 22, 29, 31, 32, 35-38, 40, 41, 43-47, 61, 64, 69, 70, 73, 77, 79
Hellenistic culture and influence, 2, 5, 15, 19, 20, 23, 29, 32, 34, 61, 63, 64
Hercules, 55, 57, 59
Hesiod, 44
Homer, 36, 38, 43, 57; *Iliad*, 8, 38, 77; *Odyssey*, 50, 62, 63, 77
Horace, 46 n. 26, 77
Hortensius, 74, 75 n. 53

Indo-European, 2, 3
Iphigeneia (Iphianassa), 37-39, 41, 47-49, 55, 62
Isokrates, 59
Italy and Italian culture, 3, 9, 33, 75, 78
Jerome, 28 n. 13, 73
Lesbia, 27, 41, 75 n. 53
Lesbius, 75 n. 53
Liber, 55, 57, 59
Livy, 5 n. 2, 46 n. 26
Lucan, 72
Lucretius (*De Rerum Natura*), 1, 2, 4, 13 n. 7, 15, 18, 21, 22, 28, 30, 33-79 *passim*
Lucullus 16, 55
Magna Mater, 52
Mamurra, 25, 64, 75 n. 53
Matius, 17 n. 10
Mediterranean world, 1, 2, 6, 13, 14
Memmius, 25, 36, 37, 55, 74, 75 n. 53, 77
Oresteia, 77
Ovid, 46 n. 26
Pansa, 17 n. 10, 18
Persius, 72
Petronius, 72
Philodemus, 18, 28, 34, 58 n. 36, 59, 63, 64, 74, 75 n. 53
Piso Caesonibus, L. Calpurnius, 18, 25, 55, 74-76
Plato, 32, 38, 55-56 n. 34, 59, 64
Platonism, 18, 63, 64
Plutarch, 58 n. 36
Pompey, 15, 16 n. 9, 25, 32 n. 17, 55, 72 n. 48, 75 n. 53, 77
Praenestine fibula, 4 n. 1
Propertius, 46 n. 26
Republic (Roman), 2-6, 8, 12-16, 18, 19, 21, 22, 24, 25, 27, 28, 30, 32, 33, 35, 56 n. 34, 63, 64, 74, 77, 79
Sallust, 5 n. 2, 16 n. 9, 17 n. 10, 19-21, 25
Sallustius, 34 n. 19, 61, 73
Sappho, 22, 23, 41
Saturnian verse, 4, 6
Scipio the Elder, 16, 63
Scipio the Younger, 31, 32
Sisyphus, 48, 63
Socrates, 32, 38, 58
Socration, 74
Stoicism, 18, 20, 29, 55, 56 n. 34, 76, 77
Suetonius, 16 n. 9, 74 n. 51
Suffenus, 26, 64
Tacitus, 13 n. 7, 72
Thucydides, 21
Torquatus, 49 n. 29, 58 n. 36, 73 n. 49, 75 n. 53

Trebatius, 17 n. 10, 18, 33 n. 17
triumph, 3, 6, 41
Venus, 37, 78

Virgil, 38, 46 n. 26, 55, 77, 78; *Eclogues*,
77; *Aeneid*, 55, 77, 78

Printed in the United States
By Bookmasters